Illustrator
Sue Fullam

Editor
Janet Cain, M. Ed

Editorial Manager
Ina Massler Levin, M.A.

Editor in Chief
Sharon Coan, M.S. Ed.

Creative Director
Elayne Roberts

Art Coordinator
Denice Adorno

Cover Artist
Denise Bauer

Product Manager
Phil Garcia

Imaging
James Edward Grace

Publisher
Mary D. Smith, M.S. Ed.

Treasury of Preschool Activities

Author

Deanna Reynolds

Teacher Created Resources, Inc.
6421 Industry Way
Westminster, CA 92683
www.teachercreated.com

©2000 Teacher Created Resources, Inc.
Reprinted, 2005
Made in U.S.A.

ISBN-1-57690-594-2

Table of Contents

Introduction

Treasury of Year-Round Preschool Activities is designed for the busy teachers, daycare workers, and parents who dedicate themselves to pre-school age children. It provides weekly activities designed to make learning fun and interesting without a lot of stress.

Treasury of Year-Round Preschool Activities is designed to be used as a year-round resource. It is organized with lesson ideas, arts and crafts, and a weekly cooking activity. The weekly lesson plans are organized by months, from September through August. This format is easy for teachers to use whether their schools are in session for the traditional nine-month calendar or for the twelve months of a year-round system.

This book contains:

Sample Schedules—These provide an example of a typical schedule for a half-day and full-day pre-school class. Teachers should adjust these to meet the needs of their students.

Overview of Monthly Lesson Plans—These plans outline a sequence for teaching letters, numbers, colors, and shapes, as well as the lessons for each month.

Cooking Rules—This lists rules for youngsters to tell them about kitchen safety and what to do before and after they cook.

General List of Kitchen Supplies—This allows teachers to organize their kitchen supplies before doing any of the cooking activities.

List of Monthly Food Supplies—The food supplies needed to complete the suggested activities are organized by month so that they may be purchased ahead of time.

Monthly Calendars—At the beginning of each section, a monthly calendar is provided. These can be used for planning purposes. You may wish to write in the activities for each month and send copies home to parents. This will help remind the parents and children about special activities and upcoming holidays. In addition, they can be reproduced and given to the children to teach them calendar skills or to allow them to chart information, such as the weather for each day.

Sharing Time—This is a time for discussions, hands-on experiences, and reading aloud. The children should be allowed to tell about personal experiences, share ideas, and ask questions.

Lesson Ideas—Thematic lessons are provided that include pattern and activity pages.

Movement Activities—The children build gross and fine motor skills while learning poems, chants, and sayings related to a specific theme.

Arts and Crafts Ideas—A variety of arts and crafts activities are suggested, giving the children experiences with a wide range of materials.

Cooking Experiences—These activities are designed to be easy for the pre-schooler to do. They correlate with the weekly theme.

Bibliography—This has been included for some suggested books to read to the children throughout the year.

Skills Index—This has been included to show what skills are being affected, such as visual discrimination, thinking, fine motor, eye to hand coordination, shape, color, and number recognition, etc.

Sample Schedules

The following is a sample schedule for morning or afternoon classes.

8:30–8:50 A.M. or 12:30–12:50 P.M.	Free Time	This can be a variety of activities. Students can work independently to put together puzzles, color pictures, read books, or participate in learning games. As the children arrive, they can use this time to put away their things and to socialize. Meanwhile, you can organize for the morning or afternoon, as well as greet the children and their parents.
8:50–9:00 A.M. or 12:50–1:00 P.M.	Clean-Up	Have students get the room back in order so the day can begin.
9:00–9:30 A.M. or 1:00–1:30 P.M.	Circle Time	Create your own activities or choose one or more of the following: recite the alphabet, count numbers, name shapes, say the Pledge of Allegiance, discuss the calendar, recite fingerplays, sing songs, or have Show-'n'-Tell.
9:30–9:45 A.M. or 1:30–1:45 P.M.	Snack Time	Snacks should be nutritious and easy to make. Limit sugary treats to special occasions. Use this time to teach students to wash their hands before eating and how to use good manners.
9:45–10:45 A.M. or 1:45–2:45 P.M.	Centers	Divide the class into three groups. Place a group at each of three centers. Rotate the groups every 20 minutes. *Center 1:* The children work with you to complete the daily lesson, art project, etc. *Center 2:* The children work independently to do hands-on activities, such as tracing, using pegboards, and creating with playdough. *Center 3:* The children work independently. They may engage in dramatic play in a kitchen or dress-up center, do reading or science activities, or build with blocks.
10:45–11:00 A.M. or 2:45 - 3:00 P.M.	Clean-Up	Have students put things away.
11:00–11:15 A.M. or 3:00–3:15 P.M.	Recess	This is usually a free-choice playtime, but it can be used to help students develop large motor skills, such as skipping and hopping; jumping rope; tossing, kicking, and catching a ball.
11:15–11:30 A.M. or 3:15–3:30 P.M.	Recall Time	This is a time to review with students what they have done that day. Take note of what worked or didn't work so you can adjust your plans accordingly. You may wish to build anticipation by telling students what activities you have prepared for the next day. Then have the children get ready to go home.

Sample Schedules (cont.)

The following is a sample schedule for all-day classes.

Time	Activity	Description
8:30–8:50 A.M.	Freetime	This can be a variety of activities. Students can work independently to put together puzzles, color pictures, read books, or participate in learning games. As the children arrive, they can use this time to put away their things and to socialize. Meanwhile, you can organize for the morning or afternoon, as well as greet the children and their parents.
8:50–9:00 A.M.	Clean-Up	Have students get the room back in order so the day can begin.
9:00–9:30 A.M.	Circle Time	Create your own activities or choose one or more of the following: recite the alphabet, count numbers, name shapes, say the Pledge of Allegiance, discuss the calendar, recite fingerplays, sing songs, or have Show-'n'-Tell.
9:30–10:45 A.M.	Centers	Divide the class into three groups. Place a group at each of three centers. Rotate the groups every 20 minutes. See page 4 for a description of the three types of centers.
10:45–11:00 A.M.	Clean-Up	Have students put things away.
11:00–11:30 A.M.	Recess Time	This is usually a free-choice playtime, but it can be used to help students develop large motor skills, such as skipping and hopping; jumping rope; tossing, kicking, and catching a ball.
11:30–11:45 A.M.	Preparing for Lunch	Wash hands and get children seated and have lunches served.
11:45–12:15 P.M.	Lunch Time	If your lunch time must be later than this, be sure to allow time for a morning snack. As children finish their lunches have them put their things away and help clean up.
12:15–12:30 P.M.	Preparing for Rest	Have mats laid out ahead of time—restrooms and drinks.
12:30–1:30 P.M.	Rest Time	Use a variety of soothing and relaxing techniques to get children to relax and rest. Examples: Don't read a story—tell a made up story in a quiet tone, play relaxing classical music, etc.
1:30–1:45 P.M.	Wake Up	Have child help put away rest things and get ready for recess.
1:45–2:00 P.M.	Recess Time	Have the children play games that relate to the theme of the morning's lesson or take them for a walk to compare and contrast mornings and afternoons.
2:00–2:45 P.M.	Freetime	Students can participate in a variety of activities, such as painting, coloring, or playing with toys.
2:45–3:00 P.M.	Recall Time	This is a time to review with students what they have done that day. Take note of what worked or didn't work so you can adjust your plans accordingly. You may wish to build anticipation by telling students what activities you have prepared for the next day. Then have the children get ready to go home.

Overview of Monthly Lesson Plans

SEPTEMBER

Letters: A, B, C

Numbers: 0, 1

Colors: Green, Blue, Red, Yellow

Shape: Circle

Week 1
   Lesson Topic: Everyone Is Special
   Cooking Experience: Me Cookies

Week 2
   Lesson Topics: Rules at School and Trains
   Cooking Experience: Train Car Cracker

Week 3
   Lesson Topic: Dinosaurs
   Cooking Experience: Excavation Pudding

Week 4
   Lesson Topic: Dinosaur Eggs and Babies
   Cooking Experience: Dinosaur Eggs

OCTOBER

Letters: D, E, F

Numbers: 2, 3

Colors: Red, Brown, Yellow, Orange, Black

Shape: Triangle

Week 1
   Lesson Topics: Changing Leaves and Teddy Bears
   Cooking Experience: Bear Claws

Week 2
   Lesson Topic: Apples
   Cooking Experience: Spiced Apples

Week 3
   Lesson Topics: Fire Prevention and Columbus Day
   Cooking Experience: Sailing Ships

Week 4
   Lesson Topic: Halloween
   Cooking Experience: Ghost and Pumpkin Cookies

Overview of Monthly Lesson Plans *(cont.)*

NOVEMBER

Letters: G, H, I

Number: 4

Colors: Red, Orange, Yellow, Brown, Blue

Shape: Rectangle

Week 1
    Lesson Topics: Owls and Squirrels
    Cooking Experience: Bologna Owls

Week 2
    Lesson Topic: Native Americans
    Cooking Experience: Marshmallow Totem Poles

Week 3
    Lesson Topic: Pilgrims
    Cooking Experience: Pumpkin Pudding

Week 4
    Lesson Topics: Thanksgiving and Turkeys
    Cooking Experience: Turkey Toast

DECEMBER

Letters: J, K, L

Number: 5

Colors: Yellow, Red, Green, Black, Pink, Brown

Shape: Star

Week 1
    Lesson Topic: Stars
    Cooking Experience: Star Cookies

Week 2
    Lesson Topics: Hanukkah and Kwanzaa
    Cooking Experience: Nutty Bananas

Week 3
    Lesson Topic: Reindeer
    Cooking Experience: Peanut Butter Reindeer

Week 4
    Lesson Topic: Gifts
    Cooking Experience: Surprise Pudding

Overview of Monthly Lesson Plans *(cont.)*

JANUARY

Letters: M, N, O

Colors: Red, Blue, White, Green, Yellow, Blue, Brown

Numbers: 6 and 7

Shape: Square

Week 1
  Lesson Topic: Hot and Cold Weather
  Cooking Experience: Hot and Cold Gelatin

Week 2
  Lesson Topic: Winter Clothing
  Cooking Experience: Snowcones

Week 3
  Lesson Topic: Snowflakes
  Cooking Experience: Sugar Snowflakes

Week 4
  Lesson Topic: Snow People
  Cooking Experience: Marshmallow Snow People

Week 5
  Lesson Topic: Inuit
  Cooking Experience: Edible Igloos

FEBRUARY

Letters: P, Q, R

Colors: Red, Green, Blue, Yellow, Pink, Purple

Number: 8

Shape: Heart

Week 1
  Lesson Topics: Groundhog Day and Shadows
  Cooking Experience: Groundhog in a Blanket

Week 2
  Lesson Topic: Post Office and Addresses
  Cooking Experience: Letters and Envelopes

Week 3
  Lesson Topic: Valentine's Day
  Cooking Experience: Queen of Hearts Tarts

Week 4
  Lesson Topic: Abraham Lincoln and George Washington
  Cooking Experience: Washington's Cherry Pie

Overview of Monthly Lesson Plans *(cont.)*

MARCH

Letters: S, T, U

Number: 9

Colors: Green, Yellow, Red, Gold

Shapes: Diamond and Shamrock

Week 1
    Lesson Topics: Winds and Phone Numbers
    Cooking Experience: Lion Salad and Lamb Cupcakes

Week 2
    Lesson Topic: St. Patrick's Day
    Cooking Experience: Green Eggs and Ham

Week 3
    Lesson Topics: Kites and Clouds
    Cooking Experience: Clouds in the Sky Pudding

Week 4
    Lesson Topic: Money
    Cooking Experience: Golden Coins

Easter Week
    Lesson Topic: Easter Egg Hunt
    Cooking Experience: Baby Chicks

APRIL

Letters: V, W, X

Number: 10

Colors: Red, Black, Silver, Green

Shape: Oval

Week 1
    Lesson Topics: Rain Showers and Rainbows
    Cooking Experience: Rainbow Pudding

Week 2
    Lesson Topics: Spring Flowers and Honeybees
    Cooking Experience: Edible Honeybees

Week 3
    Lesson Topic: Ladybugs
    Cooking Experience: Ladybug Cookies

Week 4
    Lesson Topics: Caterpillars and Butterflies
    Cooking Experience: Caterpillar Salad

Week 5
    Lesson Topic: Birds
    Cooking Experience: Birds' Nests and Eggs

Overview of Monthly Lesson Plans *(cont.)*

MAY

Letters: Y and Z
Numbers: Review

Colors: Review
Shapes: Review

Week 1
    Lesson Topic: Sunshine
    Cooking Experience: Sunshine Salad
Week 2
    Lesson Topics: Planting
    Cooking Experience: Dirt Cup and Beans
Week 3
    Lesson Topics: Growing Fruits and Vegetables
    Cooking Experience: Vegetable Bites and Dip
Week 4
    Lesson Topic: May Flowers
    Cooking Experience: Fruit Flowers

JUNE

Letters: Review
Numbers: Review

Colors: Review
Shapes: Review

Week 1
    Lesson Topics: Vacations and Transportation
    Cooking Experience: Peanut Butter Airplanes
Week 2
    Lesson Topic: Germany
    Cooking Experience: Gingerbread Houses
Week 3
    Lesson Topics: Mexico
    Cooking Experience: Quesadillas
Week 4
    Lesson Topic: Japan
    Cooking Experience: Rice Cakes

Overview of Monthly Lesson Plans *(cont.)*

JULY

Letters: Review   Colors: Review

Numbers: Review   Shapes: Review

Week 1
- Lesson Topics: Fourth of July and Fireworks
- Cooking Experience: Fourth of July Kabobs

Week 2
- Lesson Topics: Beaches and Seashells
- Cooking Experience: Gelatin Aquarium

Week 3
- Lesson Topic: Starfish and Sand Castles
- Cooking Experience: Sandcups

Week 4
- Lesson Topic: Ocean Life
- Cooking Experience: Octopus

Week 5
- Lesson Topic: Fish
- Cooking Experience: Frosted Fish

AUGUST

Letters: Review   Colors: Review

Numbers: Review   Shapes: Review

Week 1
- Lesson Topic: Farm Animals
- Cooking Experience: Pigs in Blankets

Week 2
- Lesson Topic: Fruit Harvest
- Cooking Experience: Fruit Kabobs

Week 3
- Lesson Topic: Vegetable Harvest
- Cooking Experience: Biscuits and Honey Butter

Week 4
- Lesson Topic: Back to School
- Cooking Experience: Homemade Ice Cream

Cooking Rules

Discuss the rules on this page before you attempt any recipes with children. You may wish to reproduce and display the rules on poster board.

Before You Cook

1. Wash your hands.

2. Put on an apron.

3. Read the recipe.

4. Gather the utensils and ingredients.

5. Follow the recipe steps in order.

6. Clean up as you go.

After You Cook

1. Be sure all appliances are turned off and unplugged.

2. Wash and dry all utensils.

3. Put everything away.

4. Leave everything neat and clean.

Rules for Cooking Safety

1. Let an adult help with sharp knives and hot appliances.

2. Use a cutting board to chop foods. Always cut away from your body.

3. Use pot holders for hot pots and pans.
   Keep the handles turned toward the stove.

4. Turn off and unplug appliances
   when you are finished using them.

5. Wipe up spills when they happen.

6. Roll up long sleeves.

7. Tie back long hair.

8. Cover your mouth when you sneeze or cough, and then wash your hands again.

9. Do not put food in your mouth while you are cooking.

10. Use a step stool or other steady surface to raise you to the proper height for work
    or to look for supplies.

General List of Kitchen Supplies

The following is a list of kitchen supplies that you will want to have for the cooking activities suggested in this book.

Aluminum foil

Aprons or smocks

Baking spray

Blender (For adult use only.)

Cookie sheets

Craft sticks

Food coloring

Hand soap

Large plastic bowls

Large wooden spoons

Liquid dishwashing soap

Measuring cups

Measuring spoons

Non-stick skillet

Paper bowls

Paper cups

Paper napkins

Paper plates

Paper towels

Plastic forks

Plastic knives

Plastic spoons

Plastic wrap

Potholders

Resealable plastic bags

Sharp knife (For adult use only.)

Spatulas

Toaster (For adult use only.)

Tongs

Toothpicks

Wax paper

Whisk

Other _____

_____

List of Monthly Food Supplies

September

Bananas
Chocolate chips
Chocolate instant pudding
Cookie dough (pre-made)
Eggs (hard-boiled)
Flavored powered drinks (bright colors)
Gel icing (assorted colors)
Graham crackers
Gummy dinosaurs
Mayonnaise
Milk
Peanut butter
Vinegar
Whipped topping
White icing

October

Almond slivers
Apples
Butter
Cans of biscuits
Chocolate chips
Cinnamon sugar
Colored mini-marshmallows
Dough for sugar cookies
Flour
Green gel icing
Orange food coloring
White icing

November

Bologna
Bread slices
Can of pumpkin pie filling
Cheese slices
Chocolate syrup
Fruit-flavored, o-shaped cereal
Honey
Large marshmallows
Milk
Peanut butter
Pickles (round slices)
Pumpkin spice
Red gel icing
Strawberry syrup

December

Bananas
Christmas chocolate candy
Colored sugar
Dough for sugar cookies
Flour
Green food coloring
Honey
Nut topping
Peanut butter
Powdered milk
Raisins
Red hot candies
Sesame seeds
Small pretzel knots
Vanilla instant pudding

List of Monthly Food Supplies *(cont.)*

January

Apples
Cooking oil
Flour tortillas
Frozen juice (grape, orange, etc.)
Ice cubes
Large marshmallows
Liquid chocolate syrup
Mini-marshmallows
Packages of flavored gelatin (cherry, orange, etc.)
Peanut butter
Powdered sugar

April

Almond slivers
Apples
Chocolate chips
Chocolate icing
Chocolate syrup
Colored mini-marshmallows
Dough for sugar cookies
Food coloring (various colors)
Honey
Milk
Oranges
Peanut butter
Pears
Plums
Powdered milk
Sesame seeds
Strawberries
Thin black licorice
Vanilla instant pudding

February

Can of biscuits
Can of cherry pie filling
Can of whipped cream
Hot dogs
Sliced cheese
Small flour tortillas
Strawberry preserves

March

Bananas
Butter
Can of whipped cream
Coconut
Eggs
Milk
Peach halves
Raisins
Shredded cheese
Vanilla instant pudding
Vanilla wafers
White frosted snack cakes
White ready-made icing
Easter (March or April)
Boiled eggs
Coconut
Mayonnaise
Mustard
Raisins
Vinegar

List of Monthly Food Supplies *(cont.)*

May

Bananas
Chocolate instant pudding
Chocolate sandwich cookies
Honey
Jellybeans
Kiwi
Mayonnaise
Milk
Peanut butter
Pineapple tidbits (large can)
Powdered milk
Raisins
Ranch dip mix
Sesame seeds
Strawberries
Thin licorice
Vegetables (any variety)
Whipped topping
Yogurt (banana flavored)

June

Almond slivers
Apples
Black olives
Flour tortillas
Graham crackers
Gumdrops and candy
Honey
Jelly (any flavor)
Mild salsa (optional)
Peanut butter
Powdered milk
Raisins
Rice cakes (any flavor)
Sesame seeds
Shredded cheese
Sliced fruit (any type)
Tomatoes
White icing

July

Blue gelatin
Colored sugar wafer cookies
Cupcakes (pre-made and unfrosted)
Fruit-flavored, o-shaped cereal
Gummy fish
Hot dogs
Milk
Ranch dip
Vanilla icing
Vanilla instant pudding
Vanilla wafers
Vegetables cut into chunks (any variety)

August

Cans of biscuits
Cheese slices (optional)
Chunks of fruit (your choice)
Crushed ice
Flavored extracts (cherry, peppermint, etc.)
Heavy whipping cream
Honey
Hot dogs
Milk
Sugar
Yogurt (any flavor)

Parent Letter

Dear Parent(s) of _____:

Our class will be cooking a variety of recipes. I realize that your child may have food allergies or dietary restrictions. Please write an X next to any of the foods listed below that your child cannot eat, and return this form. Thank you!

Sincerely,

_____

(Teacher)

_____ Almonds
_____ Apples
_____ Bananas
_____ Black olives
_____ Bologna
_____ Bread
Type(s): _____
_____ Butter
_____ Cake/Cupcakes
Type(s): _____
_____ Canned biscuits
_____ Carrots
_____ Celery
_____ Cheese
_____ Cherries
_____ Chocolate
_____ Cinnamon
_____ Coconut
_____ Cookies
Type(s): _____
_____ Cooking oil
_____ Cucumbers
_____ Eggs
_____ Flavored extracts
Flavor(s): _____
_____ Flour tortillas
_____ Food coloring
_____ Fruit flavored, o-shaped cereal
_____ Gelatin

Flavor(s): _____
_____ Graham crackers
_____ Granulated sugar
_____ Grapes
_____ Gumdrops
_____ Gummy candies
_____ Ham
_____ Honey
_____ Hot dogs
_____ Icing
Flavor(s): _____
_____ Juice
Flavor(s): _____
_____ Jelly
Flavor(s): _____
_____ Kiwi
_____ Licorice
_____ Marshmallows
_____ Mayonnaise
_____ Milk or milk products
_____ Mustard
_____ Nuts
_____ Oranges
_____ Peaches
_____ Peanut butter
_____ Pears
_____ Pickles
_____ Pineapple
_____ Plums

_____ Powdered milk
_____ Pudding
Flavor(s): _____
_____ Pumpkin
_____ Pumpkin spice
_____ Raisins
_____ Ranch dip
_____ Rice cakes
_____ Salsa (hot sauce)
_____ Sesame seeds
_____ Strawberries
_____ Tomatoes
_____ Vanilla wafers
_____ Vegetables
Type(s): _____
_____ Vinegar
_____ Wheat
_____ Whip cream
_____ Yogurt
Flavor(s): _____
Other(s): _____

General List of Activity Supplies

Use this list to check off what materials you currently have and to find out which ones you still need.

- ❑ Beads (assorted shapes)
- ❑ Birthday candles (assorted colors)
- ❑ Brads
- ❑ Christmas foil wrapping paper (assorted colors and patterns)
- ❑ Clothespins
- ❑ Colored pencils (assorted colors)
- ❑ Construction paper (assorted colors)
- ❑ Contact paper
- ❑ Cotton balls (assorted colors)
- ❑ Crayons (assorted colors)
- ❑ Crepe paper streamers (assorted colors)
- ❑ Cupcake holders
- ❑ Disposable pie tins
- ❑ Dried beans
- ❑ Elastic cording or lacing (assorted colors)
- ❑ Empty toilet paper holders
- ❑ Feathers (assorted colors and sizes)
- ❑ Fishing line
- ❑ Glitter (assorted colors)
- ❑ Glue
- ❑ Green pompons—1/2" (1.25 cm)
- ❑ Hole punch
- ❑ Large furniture boxes
- ❑ Large rocks (fist size)
- ❑ Magazines
- ❑ Magnets
- ❑ Markers (assorted colors)
- ❑ Movable eyes (assorted sizes)
- ❑ Paintbrushes (assorted sizes)
- ❑ Paper clips
- ❑ Pencils

- ❑ Permanent markers
- ❑ Pipe cleaners (assorted colors and sizes)
- ❑ Plaster of Paris
- ❑ Plastic cups
- ❑ Poster board (assorted colors)
- ❑ Potting soil
- ❑ Rubber bands
- ❑ Safety pins
- ❑ Safety scissors
- ❑ Sand (assorted colors)
- ❑ Sequins (assorted colors)
- ❑ Sharp scissors (adult use only)
- ❑ Small paper plates
- ❑ Small seashells (assorted colors)
- ❑ Small tree branches
- ❑ Sponges
- ❑ Stapler and staples (adult use only)
- ❑ Stickers (assorted colors and designs)
- ❑ Styrofoam balls—3" (7.5 cm); (assorted colors)
- ❑ Styrofoam cubes—3" (7.5 cm); (assorted colors)
- ❑ Styrofoam cups
- ❑ Styrofoam packing pieces
- ❑ Tempera paint (assorted colors)
- ❑ Tissue paper (assorted colors)
- ❑ Toothpicks
- ❑ Vegetable seeds (fast growing)
- ❑ Watercolors (assorted colors)
- ❑ Wide craft sticks
- ❑ Wooden stars—3" (7.5 cm)
- ❑ Yarn (assorted colors)

September

Sunday	Monday	Tuesday	Wednesday	Thursday	Friday	Saturday

Everyone Is Special!

═══════════════════ **DAY 1** ═══════════════════

Sharing Time: Talk about what makes the children special and how they feel about themselves and others. Discuss how it's special to make new friends.

Movement Activity: Have students practice "A New Friend" (page 22) all week.

Lesson: The Way to School

    Materials: crayons; copies of page 23, one per student

    Directions: Have the children trace a path from the friends to their school. Then have them finish coloring the picture.

═══════════════════ **DAY 2** ═══════════════════

Sharing Time: Provide some hand-held mirrors so the children can look at themselves. Talk about eye color, hair color and length, freckles, smiles, etc. Discuss how they are alike and how they are different.

Lesson: Look at Me, I'm Special

    Materials: colored pencils, copies of page 24

    Directions: After the children have used the mirrors, have them draw self-portraits. To get them started, draw an oval for the head. They may need to look in the mirrors as they draw.

═══════════════════ **DAY 3** ═══════════════════

Sharing Time: Have the children talk about their favorite colors, food, toys, etc. Point out how many of them like the same things.

Lesson: I Am Special Book

    Materials: crayons or colored pencils, scissors, stapler, copies of page 25

    Directions: Help students fill in the blanks to complete the sentences. Then help them put the books together by cutting apart the four pages, putting them in order, and stapling them along the left-hand side.

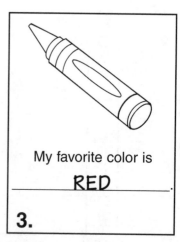

My favorite color is

RED

3.

Everyone Is Special! *(cont.)*

======================= **DAY 4** =======================

Arts and Crafts: Friendship Bracelets

   Materials: elastic cord or plastic lace, one piece per student; scissors; beads (assorted colors and shapes)

   Directions: Assign partners. Have students make a friendship bracelet for their partner. Using elastic cording or lacing, cut a piece to fit the child's wrist. Knot one end and then have the children string the beads on until it's full. Then tie the ends together and have them give each other their bracelets. Have the children trade bracelets.

======================= **DAY 5** =======================

Cooking Experience: Me Cookies

   Materials: cookie sheet; cooking spray; spatula; slice-and-bake cookie dough; frosting; chocolate chips; yellow, brown, black, and red or pink gel icing; paper plates; plastic knives

   Directions: Prepare and bake the cookies according to the directions on the package. Allow the cookies to cool. Let the children decorate the cookies to look like themselves using frosting; chocolate chips for the eyes and nose; pink or red gel icing for the mouth; and yellow, brown, red, or black gel icing for the hair. Then allow the children to enjoy eating the cookies.

A New Friend

Movement Activity

Who will be my friend?

(Shrug shoulders and shake head.)

Who will be my friend?

(Shrug shoulders and shake head.)

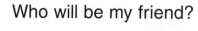

Please be my friend.

(Point to someone in the group.)

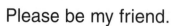

Please be my friend.

(Point to someone in the group.)

We are new friends!

(Hold hands with a new friend and smile.)

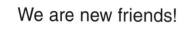

We are new friends!

(Hold hands with a new friend and smile.)

Deanna Reynolds

Name: _____ Date: _____

The Way to School

These two friends are walking to school. Trace the path they should take to get to school. Then color the picture.

Name: _____ Date: _____

Look at Me, I'm Special

Draw a picture of yourself. Color your picture.

I Am Special Book

Complete the little book. Cut apart the pages. Then have an adult staple your book together.

I Am Special

By _____

1.

My favorite food is

_____.

2.

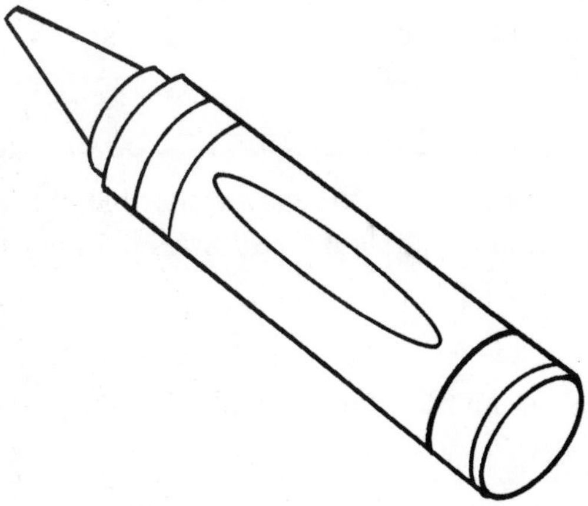

My favorite color is

_____.

3.

My favorite toy is

_____.

4.

Rules at School and Trains

═══ DAY 1 ═══

Sharing Time: Talk to the children about school and classroom rules. Explain that one of your rules is that things, such as books, toys, and trash, need to be put where they belong. Show children where specific things belong. Have them practice putting things away. You can do this with songs or by placing objects in the middle of the floor and having the children put them away.

Lesson: Where Our Things Belong

> **Materials:** crayons, copies of page 28
>
> **Directions:** Have the children draw lines from the items on the left to the place where they would be put away on the right.

═══ DAY 2 ═══

Sharing Time: Read aloud the book *The Little Engine that Could* (page 302) each day for the rest of the week. Discuss the story. If a child uses a negative phrase such as, "I can't do it," ask the child to use a positive phrase like, "I think I can." Encourage the children to think like the little engine in the story.

Movement Activity: Have students practice The Little Train (page 27) all week.

═══ DAY 3 ═══

Sharing Time: Allow students to look at a variety of books about trains. Point out that the wheels on the train cars are round. Explain that the shape of a wheel is called a circle.

Lesson: Circle Trains

> **Materials:** colored pencils, copies of page 29
>
> **Directions:** Have the children trace all of the circles on the trains. Then have them draw lines to match the trains on the left with the trains on the right. Invite them to color the trains.

═══ DAY 4 ═══

Sharing Time: Talk about trains using books, records, tapes, or movies. Whenever possible, remind children to say, "I think I can," when they express negative thoughts about their abilities.

Lesson: I Think I Can Train

> **Materials:** colored pencils, copies of page 30
>
> **Directions:** Ask the children to trace all of the circles on the train cars. Then invite them to color the train cars.

═══ DAY 5 ═══

Cooking Experience: Train Car Cracker

> **Materials:** paper plates, plastic knives, peanut butter, one whole graham cracker per child, two banana slices per child, chocolate chips
>
> **Directions:** Have the children spread peanut butter on their graham crackers. Show them how to add two banana slices for the wheels and chocolate chips for the windows of their train cars.

The Little Train

Movement Activity

The little train goes around and around the track.

(Pretend to be a train going around in a circle.)

The little train blows its whistle. Wooo! Wooo!

(Raise up one hand and pretend to pull a train whistle two times.)

The little train goes around and around the track.

(Pretend to be a train going around in a circle.)

The little train blows its whistle. Wooo! Wooo!

(Raise up one hand and pretend to pull a train whistle two times.)

Deanna Reynolds

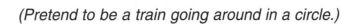

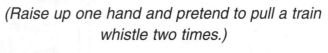

Name: _____ Date: _____

Where Our Things Belong

Draw lines from the things on the right to the place where they belong on the left.

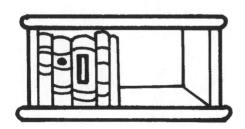

Name: _____ Date: _____

Circle Trains

Trace all the circles on the trains. Draw lines to match the trains on the right with the trains on the left if they contain circles. Then color the trains.

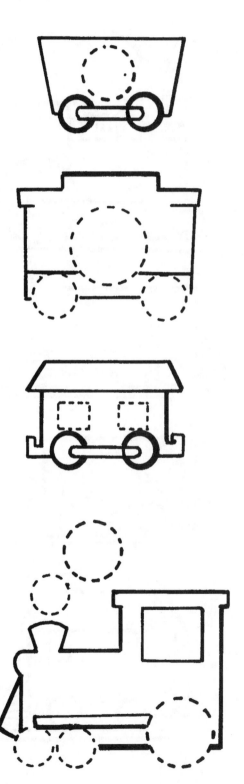

Name: _____ Date: _____

I Think I Can Train

Trace all of the circles. Color the train cars.

Dinosaurs Big and Small

═══════════════════════════ DAY 1 ═══════════════════════════

Sharing Time: Provide a variety of dinosaur books and pictures. Tell the children that the dinosaurs died out long ago. Explain that some dinosaurs were big and others were small.

Movement Activity: Have students practice "Be the Dinosaurs" (page 33) all week.

Lesson: Color the Dinosaur

   Materials: crayons, copies of page 34

   Directions: First teach students the letters A, B, and C. Then have them color the picture according to the directions.

═══════════════════════════ DAY 2 ═══════════════════════════

Sharing Time: Use toy dinosaurs to show how many 0 and 1 are.

Lesson: Dinosaur Count

   Materials: colored pencils, copies of page 35

   Directions: Have the children count how many dinosaurs are in each row, write the number 0 or 1, and color the dinosaurs.

═══════════════════════════ DAY 3 ═══════════════════════════

Sharing Time: Show a variety of toy dinosaurs for the children to compare and contrast.

Arts and Crafts: Dinosaur Bracelet

   Materials: copies of page 36, markers or crayons, scissors, tape, contact paper (optional)

   Directions: Cut apart the bracelet patterns. Let each child pick a pattern. Have the children color and cut out their bracelets. You may wish to cover the bracelets with contact paper to make them stronger. Cut the slit in each bracelet. Then use the tab and slit to fit the bracelet to the child's wrist. Tape the tab in place. Invite students to wear their bracelets.

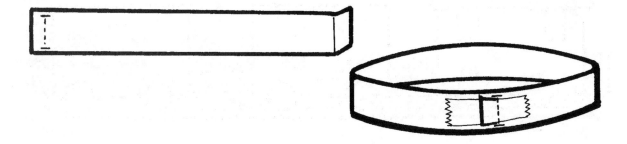

Dinosaurs Big and Small *(cont.)*

=========================== DAY 4 ===========================

Sharing Time: Tell the children about volcanoes. Explain how lava covers everything in its path when a volcano erupts. Point out that some dinosaurs probably got caught in the lava. Explain how scientists excavate to find the dinosaur bones.

Lesson: Erupting Volcano

> **Materials:** red and yellow crayons or markers, copies of page 37

> **Directions:** Have the children color the big circles red and the little ones yellow.

=========================== DAY 5 ===========================

Cooking Experience: Excavation Pudding

> **Materials:** small plastic bowls, plastic spoons, large bowl, whisk, measuring cups, 16-ounce (450 g) package of chocolate cookies, resealable plastic bag, milk, whipped topping, one large package of instant chocolate pudding per six children, gummy dinosaurs

> **Directions:** Ahead of time, crush the cookies in a resealable plastic bag. Invite the children to help make the pudding. Mix ½ of the crushed cookies and the whipped topping. Put a little of this mixture in each child's bowl. Then fill the bowls with pudding. Sprinkle a little bit of crushed cookies on top of the pudding. When the children aren't looking, hide 2-3 gummy dinosaurs in each child's pudding. Give each child a bowl. Tell children to pretend the pudding and cookies are dirt. Have them imagine they are scientists. Ask them to "excavate" their pudding.

Be the Dinosaurs

Movement Activity

Be a Brontosaurus and stomp your feet.

(Stomp feet loudly.)

Be a Pteranodon and flap your wings.

(Flap arms like wings.)

Be a Tyrannosaurs Rex and show your teeth and growl.

(Show teeth and growl loudly.)

And when I point to you, be your favorite dinosaur.

(Pretend to be your favorite dinosaur.)

Deanna Reynolds

Dinosaur Sounds

Movement Activity

Do the dinosaur stomp and stomp loudly to the right.

(Stomp loudly to the right.)

Do the dinosaur stomp and stomp quietly to the left.

(Stomp quietly to the left.)

Do the dinosaur growl and growl loudly to the right.

(Growl loudly to the right.)

Do the dinosaur growl and growl quietly to the left.

(Growl quietly to the left.)

Deanna Reynolds

Name: _____   Date: _____

Color the Dinosaur

Color the A's blue.

Color the B's green.

Color the C's yellow.

Name: _____ Date: _____

Dinosaur Count

Count the dinosaurs in each row. Write the number in the box. Then color the dinosaurs.

Name: _____ Date: _____

Dinosaur Bracelet

Cut apart the bracelet patterns. Let each child pick a pattern. Have the children color and cut out their bracelets. You may wish to cover the bracelets with contact paper to make them stronger. Cut the slits in each bracelet. Then use the tab and slits to fit the bracelet to the child's wrist. Tape the tab in place.

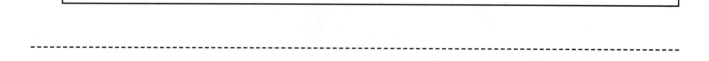

Name: _____ Date: _____

Erupting Volcano

Color the big circles red. Color the small circles yellow.

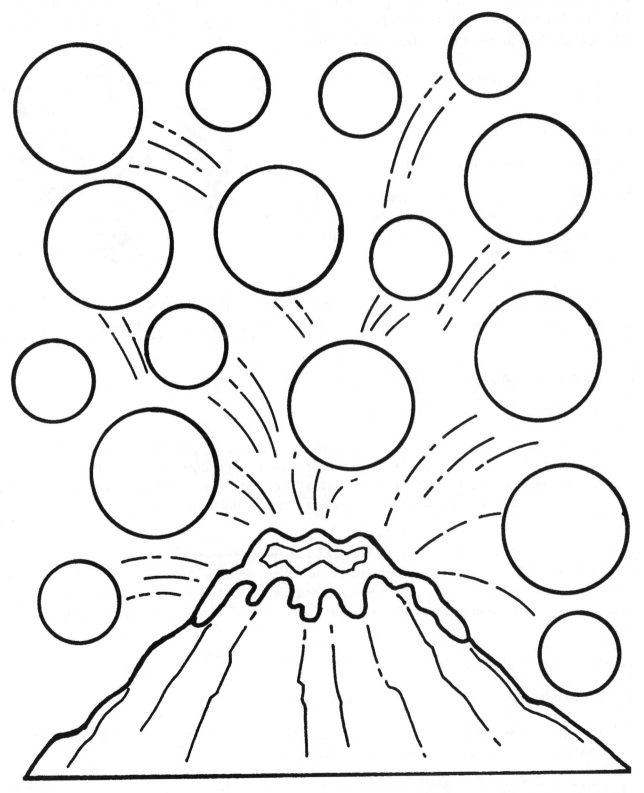

Dinosaur Eggs and Babies

DAY 1

Sharing Time: Like the previous week, have displays of toy dinosaurs, as well as books and pictures of these amazing creatures. This week's focus is on dinosaur babies being hatched from eggs. If you have a sandbox or a large tub, fill it with sand and hide plastic dinosaurs in it before the children arrive. Then let them find the plastic dinosaurs.

Movement Activity: Have students practice Dinosaur Sounds (page 33) all week.

Lesson: Find the Baby

    Materials: colored pencils or markers, copies of page 40

    Directions: Have the children draw a line from the mother dinosaur through the maze to the baby dinosaur. Point out that there is only one path that will get the mother to her baby.

DAY 2

Sharing Time: Encourage students to compare and contrast the appearance of dinosaurs, including size and color.

Lesson: Same and Different Dinosaurs

    Materials: crayons, copies of page 41

    Directions: Have the children look at the first row of dinosaurs. Ask them to find the dinosaur that is different in the first row. Tell them to write an X on the dinosaur that is different. Point out that the other dinosaurs are the same. Have the children color the dinosaurs that are the same using the same color crayon. Have the children complete the other rows in the same manner.

DAY 3

Sharing Time: Talk about the eating habits of the dinosaurs. Explain that some dinosaurs were meat-eaters, some were plant-eaters, and others ate meat and plants. Tell students that the brontosaurus was a plant-eating dinosaur. Allow students to brainstorm a list of foods that the brontosaurus might have eaten.

Lesson: Feed the Hungry Brontosaurus!

    Materials: crayons, scissors, glue, copies of page 42

    Directions: Have the children color the picture. Then have them cut out all the things that the brontosaurus would eat and glue them in the circle drawn on its stomach.

Dinosaur Eggs and Babies *(cont.)*

═══════════════════════ **DAY 4** ═══════════════════════

Sharing Time: Finish talking about how some dinosaur babies hatched from eggs.

Lesson: Hatching Baby Dinosaurs

> **Materials:** crayons or colored pencils, copies of page 43
>
> **Directions:** Have the children draw a line from each hatching baby dinosaur to its mother. Point out that the baby dinosaurs look like their mothers but are smaller. Then have the children color the pictures.

Cooking Experience: Dinosaur Eggs

This is a two-day project, with the first part being done on DAY 4 and the rest on DAY 5.

> **Materials:** one hard boiled egg per child, paper plates, plastic knives, large bowl, three packages of brightly colored powdered flavored drink mix, water, plastic wrap, mayonnaise, vinegar
>
>
>
> **Directions:** In advance, have the children mix the powered drink and water in a large bowl. Give each child a hard-boiled egg. Have the children gently crack the shell of their hard-boiled eggs all over, but do not let them peel the eggs. Next, put the cracked eggs into the bowl of drink mix. If needed, add more water to cover the eggs. Then use plastic wrap to cover the bowl. Refrigerate the bowl over night.

═══════════════════════ **DAY 5** ═══════════════════════

Cooking Experience: Dinosaur Eggs *(cont.)*

> **Materials:** one hard-boiled egg per child, paper plates, plastic knives, large bowl, three packages of brightly colored powdered flavored drink mix, water, plastic wrap, mayonnaise, vinegar
>
>
>
> **Directions:** Remove the bowl from the refrigerator and drain the drink mix. Give each child a cracked egg on a paper plate. Ask them to peel their eggs to see what kinds of designs the drink mix has left. Next have the children cut their eggs in half and put the yolks into a bowl. Add a small amount of vinegar and mayonnaise to the bowl. Then stir the mixture together. If the mixture is too dry, add some additional vinegar and mayonnaise. However, be sure to keep it thick enough to be spooned onto the children's plates. Place a spoonful on each child's plate. Instruct the children to fill their egg halves with the mixture.

Name: _____ Date: _____

Find the Baby

Help the mother brontosaurus find her baby.

Name: _____ Date: _____

Same and Different Dinosaurs

Look at the dinosaurs in each row. Write an X on the dinosaur that is different.
Then color the dinosaurs that are the same.

Name: _____ Date: _____

Feed the Hungry Brontosaurus!

A brontosaurus eats plants. Cut out the things at the bottom of the page that the brontosaurus eats. Glue those things inside the circle.

Name: _____ Date: _____

Hatching Baby Dinosaurs

Baby dinosaurs look like their parents, only smaller. Draw a line from each hatching baby dinosaur to its mother. Color the pictures.

October

Sunday	Monday	Tuesday	Wednesday	Thursday	Friday	Saturday

Changing Leaves and Teddy Bears

DAY 1

Sharing Time: This week, display books about bears, the fall season, and the changing colors of leaves. Take students on a nature walk. Tell them to look at the leaves on the trees. Ask them to name the colors of the leaves. If you do not live in an area where there is a dramatic change in the colors of the leaves, show the class pictures of trees with leaves that have changed colors. Allow the children to collect some of the leaves that have fallen off the trees.

Arts and Crafts: Leaf Suncatcher

Materials: 4" (10 cm) circles cut from contact paper, two per child; glitter; yarn; hole punch; leaves

Directions: Distribute the contact paper circles. Help the children peel off the paper backing from one circle. Lay the circles on the table, sticky side up. Have each child place a few leaves on the contact paper. Have the children sprinkle glitter everywhere except the edges. Then help them peel off the paper backing from the other circle. Have them place the second circle on top of the first, sticky sides together. Trim the edges to align them. Be sure to press along the edges of the circles to seal them. Punch a hole near the edge of each suncatcher and string yarn through it. Use the yarn to hang the suncatchers in a window.

DAY 2

Sharing Time: Have the children tell about the changes that occur during the fall, such as different leaf colors, cooler temperatures, flowers dying.

Arts and Crafts: Fall Colors

Materials: 1" (2.5 cm) square sponges; red, brown, orange, and yellow tempera paint; aluminum pie pans; copies of page 48; clothespins (optional)

Directions: Pour one color of tempera paint into each pie pan. Place sponges next to each pan. You may wish to attach clothespins to the sponges to use as holders. This will help keep the children's fingers cleaner. Show the children how to make leaf prints on the tree pattern (page 48) by dipping a sponge into some tempera paint and pressing the sponge on the paper. Then allow them to use the different colored paints to add fall leaves to their trees.

Changing Leaves and Teddy Bears *(cont.)*

DAY 3

Sharing Time: Ahead of time, invite the children to bring their favorite teddy bears for the rest of the week. Remind students to bring only one teddy bear. Have a few extras on hand for students who don't have a teddy bear. Teach the numbers 2 and 3. If possible, watch the video or read the book *Teddy Bear's Picnic* by Jimmy Kennedy. Let the children have a picnic with their bears.

Movement Activity: Have students practice "Teddy Bear, Teddy Bear" (page 47) for the rest of the week.

Lesson: Teddy Bear Numbers

   Materials: markers or colored pencils, copies of page 49

   Directions: Have the children draw two eyes and three buttons on their teddy bears. Then have them trace the 2s and 3s and write more of these numbers by themselves.

DAY 4

Sharing Time: Have the children practice writing the numbers 0-3 on the chalkboard. Have a teddy bear parade during which the children march around the school to show everyone their favorite teddy bears.

Lesson: Matching Numbers

   Materials: crayons or colored pencils, copies of page 50

   Directions: Have the children trace the numbers on the teddy bears and the honey pots. Have them cut out the honey pots and glue the honey pot onto the teddy bear's hand with the matching number. Students may wish to color the teddy bears and honey pots.

DAY 5

Cooking Experience: Bear Claws

   Materials: paper plates, cookie sheet, spray oil, cans of biscuits, brown sugar, almond slivers

   Directions: Give each child a biscuit and paper plate. Tell the children to slightly flatten and stretch the biscuit. Let each child have three almond slivers to place on top of the biscuits so they look like the claws of a bear. Sprinkle the "bear claws" with brown sugar. Put the biscuits on a cookie sheet sprayed with oil. Then bake the biscuits in an oven at 350 degrees Fahrenheit (175 degrees Celsius) for 8-10 minutes. Allow the biscuits to cool. Invite students to eat the "bear claws" with their teddy bears.

Teddy Bear, Teddy Bear

Movement Activity

Teddy Bear, Teddy Bear turn around.

(Turn around in place.)

Teddy Bear, Teddy Bear touch the ground.

(Touch the ground with hands.)

Teddy Bear, Teddy Bear reach up high.

(Stand on tiptoes, stretch out arms above head, and reach.)

Teddy Bear, Teddy Bear touch the sky.

(Pretend to touch the sky.)

Teddy Bear, Teddy Bear bend down low

(Bend over at waist.)

Teddy Bear, Teddy Bear touch your toes.

(Touch toes with hands.)

Traditional

Name: _____ Date: _____

Fall Colors

Add fall-colored leaves to the tree.

Name: _____ Date: _____

Teddy Bear Numbers

The X's on the teddy bear's face show where its eyes go. Draw two eyes for the teddy bear. The X's on the teddy bear's stomach show where its buttons go. Draw three buttons for the teddy bear.

Trace the 2s. Then write some by yourself.

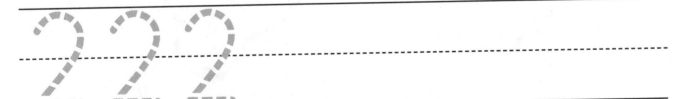

Trace the 3s. Then write some by yourself.

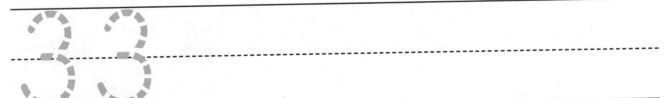

Name: _____ Date: _____

Matching Numbers

Trace the numbers on the teddy bears and the honey pots. Cut out the honey pots. Match the numbers on the honey pots with the numbers on the teddy bears. Then glue each honey pot onto the correct teddy bear's hand.

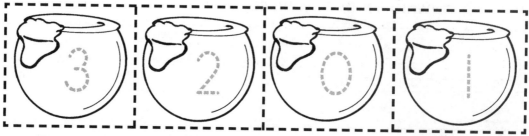

Apples

═══════════════════════ **DAY 1** ═══════════════════════

Sharing Time:

Lesson: How Many Apples?

   Materials: crayons or colored pencils, copies of page 54

   Directions: Have the children count how many apples are shown on each tree. Tell them to trace the numbers on the trees. Ask them to practice writing the four numbers by themselves. Encourage them to color the picture.

═══════════════════════ **DAY 2** ═══════════════════════

Sharing Time: Invite students to tell what they know about apples and apple trees. You may wish to provide different kinds of apples as snacks for rest of this week. Point out that apples come in different colors. Talk about the sequence of events that occur before an apple is ready to eat: (1) apple buds, or flowers, bloom; (2) little apples appear; (3) apples grow bigger; (4) apples ripen; (5) apples are picked.

Movement Activity: Have students practice "The Apple Tree" (page 53) all week.

Lesson: Three Little Apples

   Materials: crayons, colored pencils, scissors, glue, copies of page 55

   Directions: Have the children cut out the apples from the bottom of the page. Tell them to glue three of the apples onto the tree. Allow them to color the three apples and the tree. Then have them trace the 3s and write some by themselves.

═══════════════════════ **DAY 3** ═══════════════════════

Sharing Time: Read aloud stories about worms, such as *The Big Fat Worm* by Nancy Van Laan (Knopf, 1987). Explain that worms are sometimes found in apples. Invite students to tell about experiences with worms.

Lesson: Apple and Worm Patterns

   Materials: scissors, red and green construction paper, yarn, hole punch, copies of page 56

   Directions: The teacher, daycare worker, or parent needs to cut out two apples per child from red construction paper and then punch holes around the apples and let the children lace the two together with yarn. The teacher needs to cut two slits in the middle of the apple to place the worm. Let the children paint the worm green and cut out and put the worm through the red apple.

Apples *(cont.)*

DAY 4

Sharing Time: Show students an apple. Tell them that there is a surprise inside every apple. Pass around the apple for students to examine. Invite them to guess what is inside. Then cut the apple horizontally around the center to reveal a star pattern inside. Point out that this is the core of the apple, where the seeds are.

Arts and Crafts: Painting with Apples

Materials: eight metal forks, red and green tempera paint, aluminum pie tins, four apples, sharp knife, copies of page 57

Directions: Cut four apples horizontally around the center to reveal the star pattern made by the cores. Poke a fork into the end of each apple. Pour the tempera paint into the pie tins. Put four apple halves next to each paint tin. Show the children how to hold the fork to dip the apple into the red or green tempera paint. Then demonstrate how to stamp the apple as many times as needed to fill in the pattern (page 57).

DAY 5

Cooking Experience: Spiced Apples

Materials: skillet, large spoon or spatula, plastic spoons, paper plates, peeler, sharp knife, six apples, butter, cinnamon, sugar

Directions: Peel the apples and slice into thin pieces. Melt the butter in the skillet over a low heat. Then add the apples. Use the large spoon or spatula to flip the apple slices. Cook the apple slices until they are soft. Place the cooked apples on paper plates. Sprinkle with cinnamon and sugar. Allow the apples to cool before serving them to the students.

The Apple Tree

Movement Activity

Way up high in the apple tree

(Point up high.)

Two little apples smiled at me.

(Show two fingers and smile.)

I shook that tree as hard as I could.

(Pretend to shake a tree.)

Down came the apples.

(Use fingers to show apples falling down.)

Mmmm were they good!

(Rub stomach and lick lips.)

Traditional

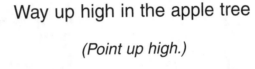

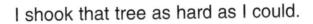

Name: _____ Date: _____

How Many Apples?

Count the apples on each tree. Trace the numbers on the tree to show how
many apples are on each tree. Color the picture.

Name: _____ Date: _____

Three Little Apples

Cut out the apples below. Glue three of them onto the tree. Color the three apples and the tree.

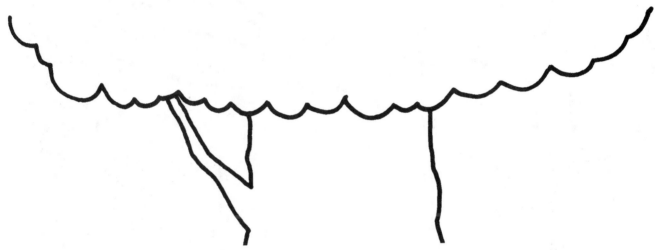

Trace the 3s. Then write some by yourself.

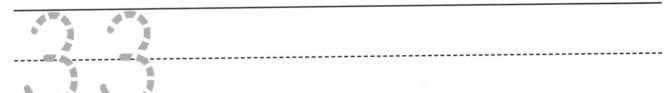

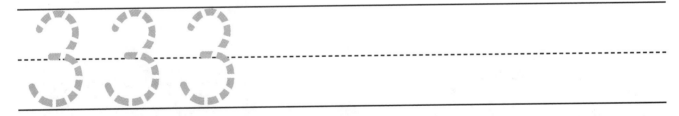

Apple and Worm Patterns

Cut apple patterns from red construction paper, two per child. Hold each set of apple patterns together so that they are aligned and punch holes around the edge. Give each child a length of yarn. Show the children how to lace the two apples together. Cut the slits in the apples for the children. Cut the worm patterns from green construction paper, one per child. Have the children slide the worm through the slits.

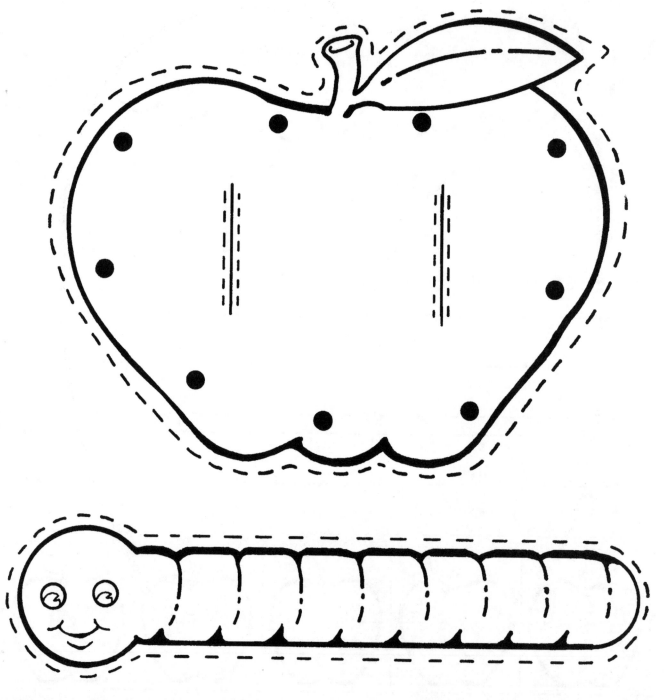

Name: _____   Date: _____

Painting with Apples

Dip the real apple into the paint to make an apple stamp. Then use the apple stamp to fill in the apple pattern shown below.

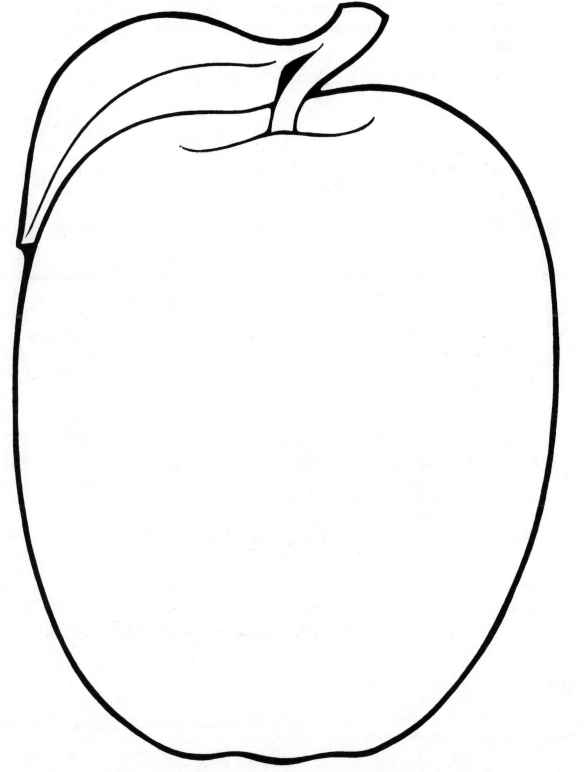

Fire Prevention and Columbus Day

━━━━━━━━━━━━━━━━━━━━━━ **DAY 1** ━━━━━━━━━━━━━━━━━━━━━━

Sharing Time: Teach the children about fire safety and fire prevention. If possible, take a field trip to a fire station to learn about fire trucks and firefighters. If this is not possible, you may be able to invite a firefighter to speak to your class.

Movement Activity: Have students practice "Firefighters" (page 60) for the next three days

Lesson: Fire Trucks

> **Materials:** red crayons or markers, copies of page 61

> **Directions:** Have the children trace the 3s and write some by themselves. Ask students to identify the numbers on the fire trucks. Tell them to use the red crayons or markers to color the fire trucks that have the number 3 on them. Ask students how many fire trucks have the number 3 on them. If students have difficulty, show them that there are three fire trucks with the number 3 on them.

━━━━━━━━━━━━━━━━━━━━━━ **DAY 2** ━━━━━━━━━━━━━━━━━━━━━━

Sharing Time: On this day, teach the children how to exit the building in case of a fire. Use a volunteer to demonstrate the stop, drop, and roll procedure. Explain that they should do this if they ever catch on fire. Stress that the worst thing they could do is to run. Practice having regular fire drills, some that are announced ahead of time and some that are not.

Lesson: Junior Firefighter Badges

> **Materials:** markers; scissors; glue; glitter; safety pins; clear contact paper (optional); copies of page 62, one copy for every four students

> **Directions:** Cut along the dotted lines to separate the badges. Give each child a badge to color. Have them smear glue on the border around the badges. Then have them sprinkle glitter onto the glue. Allow the glue to dry. Ask them to shake off any excess glitter. You may wish to use contact paper to make the badges more durable. Use safety pins to attach the badges to the children's clothing. Encourage the children to wear their badges.

━━━━━━━━━━━━━━━━━━━━━━ **DAY 3** ━━━━━━━━━━━━━━━━━━━━━━

Sharing Time: Teach the letters D, E, and F—both uppercase and lowercase. Review the letters A, B, and C. Allow students to write the uppercase and lowercase letters (A–F) on the chalkboard.

Lesson: Matching Letters

> **Materials:** colored pencils, copies of page 63

> **Directions:** Have the children use colored pencils to draw lines that show which uppercase and lowercase letters go together in each box.

Fire Prevention and Columbus Day *(cont.)*

DAY 4

Sharing Time: Columbus Day is October 12. However, it is often celebrated on a Monday. Adjust your schedule so that this activity is completed before or on Columbus Day. Tell the children about Christopher Columbus and his accomplishments. Point out that Christopher Columbus named the people he found already living in the New World "Indians," because he thought he had traveled to India. Explain that there were many different tribes, or groups, living all over the Americas. Today we call these people Native Americans. Use a world map or globe to show students where the Americas and India are. In addition, show students that Columbus started his journey from Spain.

Movement Activity: Have students practice "Christopher Columbus" (page 60).

Lesson: Christopher Columbus

   Materials: colored pencils or markers, copies of page 64

   Directions: Have the children trace the lines from each of Columbus's ships—*Niña, Pinta,* and *Santa Maria*—to a map of the New World. Next have them color the ships and the maps.

DAY 5

Cooking Experience: Columbus's Ships

   Materials: paper plates, toothpicks, colored mini-marshmallows, apples, sharp knife

   Directions: Discuss how to use toothpicks safely. Cut the apples into wedges. Give each child three apple wedges, nine toothpicks, and 27 mini-marshmallows on a paper plate. Show students how to place the apples so that the skin is touching the paper plate. Tell students to slide three mini-marshmallows onto each toothpick. The marshmallows should be placed toward one end of the toothpick with spaces in between. Then have the children place the ends without the marshmallows into the apple wedges. There should be three toothpicks in each wedge.

Firefighters

Movement Activity

Firefighters
Firefighters race to the fire.
(Run in place.)
Fire trucks turn to the left.
(Turn to the left)
Fire trucks turn to the right.
(Turn to the right.)
Firefighters put out the fire.
(Pretend to squirt water.)
Firefighters go back to the firehouse to sleep.
(Pretend to sleep.)

Deanna Reynolds

Christopher Columbus

Movement Activity

Christopher Columbus sailed in three ships —
(Pretend with hand to sail on the ocean.)
The *Niña*, the *Pinta*, and the *Santa Maria*.
(Put one finger up for each ship.)
Christopher Columbus sailed the ocean blue
(Pretend with hand to sail on the ocean.)
Until he landed in the New World in 1492.
(Hold both hands palms up.)

Deanna Reynolds

Name: _____ Date: _____

Fire Trucks

Color the three fire trucks that have the number 3 on them.

Trace the 3s. Then write some by yourself.

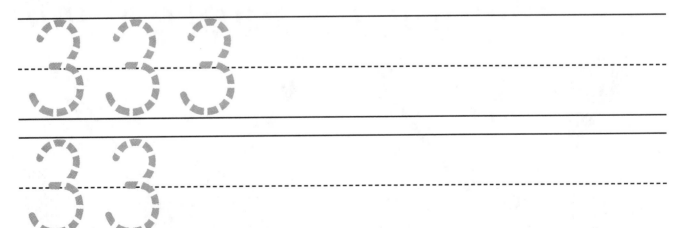

Name: _____ Date: _____

Junior Firefighter Badge

Give each child a badge. Ask the children to color and cut out their badges. Use safety pins to attach the badges to the children's clothing.

Junior Firefighter

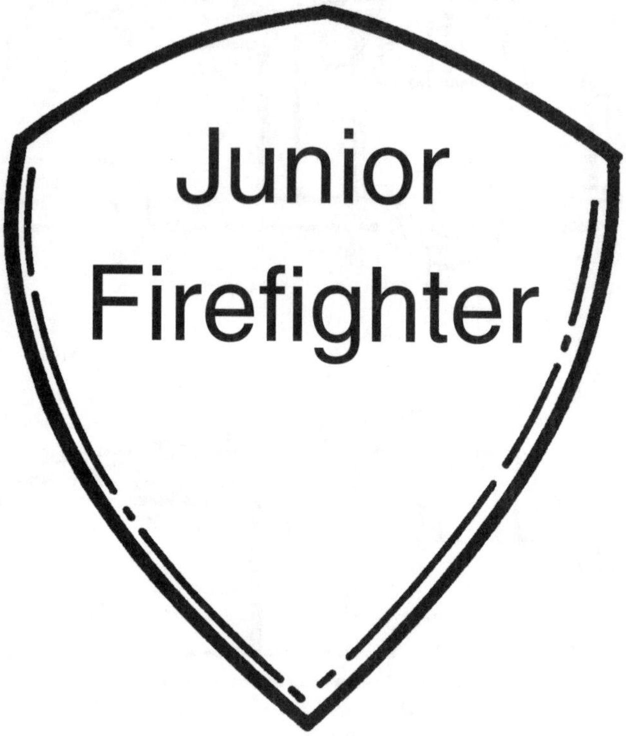

Junior Firefighter

Junior Firefighter

Junior Firefighter

Name: _____ Date: _____

Matching Letters

Draw lines to match the uppercase and lowercase letters in each box. The first one is done for you.

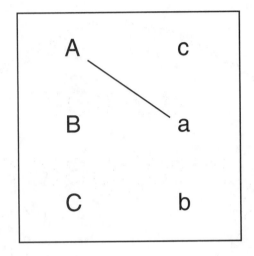

A	c
B	a
C	b

D	e
E	f
F	d

C	c
E	b
B	e

F	e
E	d
D	f

C	d
D	a
A	c

F	b
E	e
B	f

Name: _____ Date: _____

Christopher Columbus

Christopher Columbus found the New World. Trace the lines from Christopher Columbus's three ships to the maps that show the New World. Then color the ships and the maps.

Halloween, Ghosts, and Pumpkins

═══════════════════════ **DAY 1** ═══════════════════════

Sharing Time: Halloween week can be fun, but it should also be a time of learning. Some Halloween suggestions include holiday-related games, stories, songs, arts and crafts, as well as having a costume party. Introduce the shape of the triangle. Invite volunteers to point out objects in the classroom that have the triangle shape somewhere on them. You may wish to carve a real jack-o'-lantern. Cut triangles for the eyes and the nose. Guide students to describe each triangle as having three sides and three corners.

Movement Activity: Have students practice "Five Little Pumpkins" (page 67).

Lesson: Counting Jack-O'-Lanterns

   Materials: orange and yellow crayons or colored pencils, copies of page 68

   Directions: Have students practice tracing and writing the number 3. Next, have them color all of the triangle eyes and noses on the jack-o'-lanterns yellow. Then have them color three of the jack-o'-lanterns orange.

═══════════════════════ **DAY 2** ═══════════════════════

Sharing Time: Review the numbers 0–3 using the Halloween theme. For example, you could ask students to make groups of 0, 1, 2, and 3 Halloween objects such as candies.

Lesson: How Many?

   Materials: colored pencils or markers, copies of page 69

   Directions: Have the children look at each row. Read the text aloud. Ask the children to count the pictures in each row. Then have them circle the numbers that show how many pictures there are in each row. Encourage them to color the pictures.

═══════════════════════ **DAY 3** ═══════════════════════

Sharing Time: Talk about Halloween and ghosts. Remember that ghosts can be a frightening topic for this age group. Stress to the children that this is a time when people like to dress up and pretend to be scary things such as ghosts. To ease children's fears, demonstrate what a ghost might look like by throwing a white tissue into the air. Tell students to watch the tissue float to the ground. Invite volunteers to take turns floating the tissue ghost.

Movement Activity: Have students practice "The Ghost" (page 67).

Lesson: Floating Ghosts

   Materials: markers, copies of page 70

   Directions: Have the children draw lines from the ghosts on the left to the matching ghosts on the right.

Halloween, Ghosts, and Pumpkins *(cont.)*

═══════════════════ **DAY 4** ═══════════════════

Sharing Time: Have a Halloween Party or Fall Festival. This needs to be held close to October 31st or at the end of the week as chosen here. Allow the children to play games, create crafts, and participate in activities. Game suggestions: (1) Draw and cut out a ghost from white poster board and/or a jack-o'-lantern from orange poster board. Teach the children how to play Pin the Nose on the Ghost and/or Pin the Nose on the Jack-O'-Lantern. (2) Provide 3-5 plastic jack-o'-lanterns and 3–5 beanbags. Place the jack-o'-lanterns a small distance apart on the floor. Use colored tape or chalk to make a line behind which participants must stand. Have the children stand behind the designated line and toss three bean-bags into the jack-o'-lanterns. Tell them to count how many beanbags they get into the jack-o'-lanterns. Craft suggestions: Have students make ghost windsocks as described below. Activity sugges-tion: Organize a parade during which the children can wear their costumes.

Arts and Crafts: Ghost Windsocks

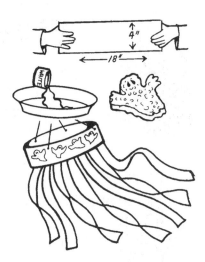

> **Materials:** orange poster board, yarn, stapler, hole punch, glue, white tempera paint, sponges cut to look like ghosts, white streamers, scissors, aluminum pie tins
>
> **Directions:** Cut a 4" x 18" (10 cm x 45 cm) strip of poster board for each child. Pour white tempera paint into the pie tins. Place the ghost-shaped sponges next to the paint. Have the children dip the ghost-shaped sponges in the paint. Then have them stamp the sponge on their strips of poster board. Allow the paint to dry. Cut 6–8 white streamers, each 24" (60 cm) long. Have the chil-dren glue the streamers onto the side of the poster board that does not have the ghost stamps on it. Staple together the two ends of each strip of poster board. Punch four holes evenly spaced near the edge at the top. String yarn through the holes. Then tie the piece of yarn together. Use the yarn to hang the windsocks.

═══════════════════ **DAY 5** ═══════════════════

Cooking Experience: Ghost and/or Pumpkin Cookies

> **Materials:** cookie sheet, spatula, rolling pin, cutting board, pumpkin and/or ghost cookie cutters, paper plates, plastic knives, spray oil, flour, pre-made sugar cookie dough, orange food coloring, canned white icing, chocolate chips, green gel icing
>
> **Directions:** Pre-heat the oven to 350° Fahrenheit (175° Celsius). Roll out the cookie dough using the cutting board, rolling pin, and flour. Let the children use the cookie cutters to make pumpkin and/or ghost cookies. You may wish to have each child make one cookie or one of each shape. Place the cookies on an oiled cookie sheet and bake for 8 to 10 minutes. Allow the cookies to cool. Have the children frost their cookies. Use orange food coloring in some of the white icing; spread the results onto the pumpkin cookies. Use chocolate chips for the face features on the ghost and pumpkins. Use green gel for the stem of the pumpkin.

The Ghost

Movement Activity

See my great big scary eyes.
(Open eyes wide.)
Look out now for a big surprise.
(Look surprised.)
OOOOOOOOO!
(Make sound like the wind.)
I'm looking right at you.
(Point to someone.)
Boo! Boo! Boo! Boo!
(Say "Boo" loudly while pointing.)

Traditional

Five Little Pumpkins

Movement Activity

Five little pumpkins sitting on a gate.
(Hold up five fingers.)
The first one said, "Oh my it's getting late!"
(Hold up index finger.)
The second one said, "There are witches in the air."
(Hold up two fingers. Point to the air.)
The third one said, "I don't care."
(Hold up three fingers. Shrug shoulders.)
The fourth one said, "Let's run, run, run."
(Hold up four fingers. Run in place.)
The fifth one said, "It's Halloween fun."
(Hold up five fingers.)
Then wooooooooo went the wind.
(Sway in place like it's windy.)
And out went the light!
(Clap hands loudly.)
Five little pumpkins rolled out of sight.
(Roll hands.)

Traditional

Name: _____ Date: _____

Counting Jack-O'-Lanterns

Color all of the triangles yellow. Color three of the jack-o'-lanterns orange.

Trace the 3s. Then write some by yourself.

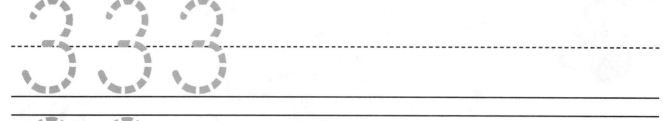

Name: _____ Date: _____

How Many?

Circle the number that answers each question. Then color the pictures.

1. Count the jack-o'-lanterns.
   How many jack-o'-lanterns are there?   0   1   2   3

2. Count the witches.
   How many witches are there?   0   1   2   3

3. Count the skeletons.
   How many skeletons are there?   0   1   2   3

4. Count the Halloween bags.
   How many Halloween bags are there?   0   1   2   3

Name: _____ Date: _____

Floating Ghosts

Draw lines from the ghosts on the left to the matching ghosts on the right.

November

	Sunday	Monday	Tuesday	Wednesday	Thursday	Friday	Saturday

Owls and Squirrels

═══ DAY 1 ═══

Sharing Time: This week discuss owls, squirrels, and how animals store food for the winter. Provide books about these topics. You may also want to include hibernation in your discussions.

Lesson: Storing Food

    Materials: markers or crayons, copies of page 74

    Directions: Have students draw lines to match the number of acorns that each squirrel has with the number of acorns in each circle. Then encourage them to color the pictures.

═══ DAY 2 ═══

Sharing Time: Talk about how squirrels hide their nuts so they can eat them during the winter. Explain that sometimes they forget where the nuts are hidden. Some of the nuts that are left behind by the squirrels grow into trees.

Lesson: Nut Hunt

    Materials: markers or colored pencils, copies of page 75

    Directions: Have the children find and circle the four nuts. Then have them color the picture. At the bottom of the page, ask students to trace the 4s and write some by themselves.

═══ DAY 3 ═══

Sharing Time: Today talk about owls and how they search for food at night.

Movement Activity: Have students practice "The Little Owl" (page 73) the rest of the week.

Arts and Crafts: Owl Pattern

    Materials: scissors, hole punch, yarn, colored poster board, copies of page 76

    Directions: Trace the pattern (page 76) onto poster board, one per child. Cut out the poster board owls. If possible, let the children help punch holes around the edge of the patterns. Then have the children use yarn to lace the owls.

═══ DAY 4 ═══

Sharing Time: Introduce the number 4 to students.

Lesson: Owl Counting

    Materials: colored pencils, copies of page 77

    Directions: Have the children count the owls in each box and circle the correct number. Allow them to color the owls. Then have them trace the 4s and write some by themselves.

═══ DAY 5 ═══

Cooking Experience: Bologna Owl

    Materials: paper plates; plastic knife; round bologna, one slice per child; round pickle slices, two per child; cheese slices, one per child

    Directions: Cut the cheese into a small triangle and a large triangle. Have children create owls using the bologna as the head, two pickles for the eyes, small triangular piece of cheese for the beak, and a large triangular piece of cheese for the top of the head.

The Little Owl

Movement Activity

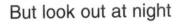

The little owl sits high in a tree.

(Point up high with one finger.)

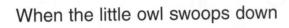

The little owl sleeps all day and never makes a sound.

(Pretend to be asleep.)

But look out at night

(Open eyes wide and look around.)

When the little owl swoops down

(Swoop with arms.)

And says "Who, who," to you.

(Say, "Who, who," and point to someone.)

Deanna Reynolds

Name: _____ Date: _____

Storing Food

Count the number of acorns that each squirrel has. Count the number of acorns in each circle. Draw lines to match the number of acorns that each squirrel has with the number of acorns in each circle. Then color the pictures.

Name: _____   Date: _____

Nut Hunt

Find and circle 4 nuts. Color the picture.

Trace the 4s. Then write some by yourself.

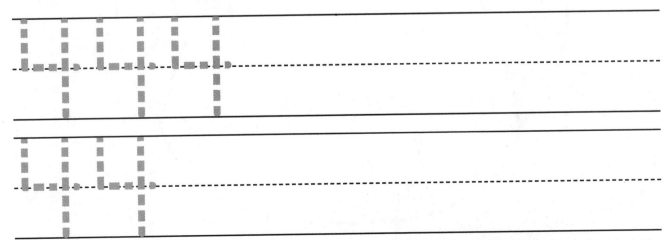

Name: _____ Date: _____

Owl Pattern

For each student, trace an owl pattern onto poster board. Cut out the owl patterns. Help the children punch holes around the edge of their patterns. Give each student a long piece of yarn. Use an owl to demonstrate how to tie one end of the yarn onto a hole in the pattern. Show the children how to lace the owl with the yarn. Then have them lace their owls.

Name: _____ Date: _____

Owl Counting

Count the owls in each box. Circle the number that shows how many owls are in the box. Then color the owls.

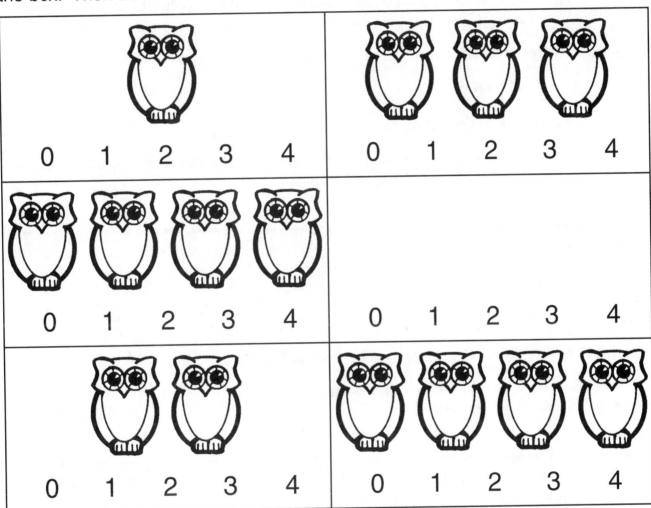

Trace the 4s. Then write some by yourself.

Native Americans

DAY 1

Sharing Time: Start talking about Native Americans and how they helped the Pilgrims through the first cold winter. Talk about their homes, their customs, and their lifestyles. Display books related to these topics. Allow time for the children to look at the books.

Movement Activity: Have students practice "The First Thanksgiving" (page 80) all week.

Lesson: Find the Way Home

   Materials: markers, copies of page 81

   Directions: Have the children use markers to trace a path from the Native American to his teepee. Point out that there is only one path that will get the boy home.

DAY 2

Sharing Time: Continue talking about the teepees in which some Native Americans once lived. If possible, set up a small tent inside or outside of your classroom. Invite the children to eat their snacks or look at books while sitting inside the tent.

Lesson: Teepee Letters

   Materials: markers or colored pencils, copies of page 82

   Directions: Have the children draw lines to match the uppercase letters with the lowercase letters.

DAY 3

Sharing Time: Tell the children that some Native Americans made totem poles to tell all kinds of stories, including ones about their family histories.

Arts and Crafts: Totem Pole

   Materials: watercolors; scissors; glitter, various colors; glue; blow dryer (optional); copies of page 83

   Directions: Have the children paint the totem poles with watercolors. Allow the paint to dry, or use a blow dryer to dry them. Have the children cut them out. Tell them to smear glue and sprinkle glitter where they want to decorate the totem poles. Then glue A to B together so the totem pole will stand up.

Native Americans *(cont.)*

================================ **DAY 4** ================================

Sharing Time: Point out that some Native Americans make sand paintings to tell stories.

Arts and Crafts: Sand Painting

Materials: white poster board, one per child; paper cutter; scissors; glue; cotton swabs; magnets, two per child; small paper plates; colored sand, a variety of colors; hot glue gun; copies of page 84

Directions: Mount the sand painting patterns onto pieces of poster board. Use a paper cutter to cut around the edges of each pattern. Pour some glue onto the paper plates. Have the children dip cotton swabs into the glue. Show them how to smear glue in the areas where they want to place a particular color of sand. Warn them to do one color at a time so that the colors do not get mixed. Tell them that after they apply each color of sand, they should shake off any excess. Have them continue smearing glue and sprinkling sand until the entire pattern is completed. Allow the glue to dry thoroughly. Use a hot glue gun to attach two magnets to the back of the sand painting. Encourage students to hang their sand paintings on the refrigerator at home.

================================ **DAY 5** ================================

Cooking Experience: Marshmallow Totem Poles

Materials: large marshmallows, toothpicks, peanut butter, chocolate and strawberry syrup, paper plates, plastic knives, spoon

Directions: On each paper plate, put a spoonful of peanut butter, three large marshmallows, and some chocolate and strawberry syrup. Give each child a plastic knife to use when spreading peanut butter on the bottom of each marshmallow. Have students connect the marshmallows by pushing them together. Tell them to place the marshmallows on the paper plate so they are standing up. Point out that the stacked marshmallows look like totem poles. Discuss using toothpicks safely. Next distribute the toothpicks to students, one per child. Let the children use the toothpicks and the chocolate and strawberry syrup to paint stories on their marshmallow totem poles.

The First Thanksgiving

Movement Activity

The Pilgrims sailed the ocean.

(Move arms to look like a ship sailing on the ocean.)

Then they settled in the new land.

(Open both hands, palms up.)

The Pilgrims met the Native Americans.

(Have fingers on both hands meet.)

Together they planted and hunted.

(Pretend to plant seeds and shoot a bow and arrow.)

Then they shared the First Thanksgiving meal.

(Pretend to eat a meal.)

Deanna Reynolds

Name: _____ Date: _____

Find the Way Home

Trace a path to show how the Native American gets home to his teepee.

Name: _____ Date: _____

Teepee Letters

All of the teepees have letters on them. Some of the letters are uppercase, or capital letters. Some of the letters are lowercase, or little letters. Draw lines to match the uppercase letters to the lowercase letters.

Totem Pole

Paint the totem pole. Let the paint dry. Cut out the totem pole. Decorate it using glue and glitter. Shake off the extra glitter. Roll A toward B. Then glue A and B together.

Sand Painting Pattern

Pilgrims

DAY 1

Sharing Time: Start this week talking about the Pilgrims who left England, sailed on a ship called the Mayflower, and landed at Plymouth Rock. Describe how the Native Americans helped the newcomers plant and grow food and taught them how to hunt. Display a variety of books and pictures related to the Pilgrims.

Movement Activity: Have students practice "The First Thanksgiving" (page 80) all week.

Lesson: Plymouth Rock

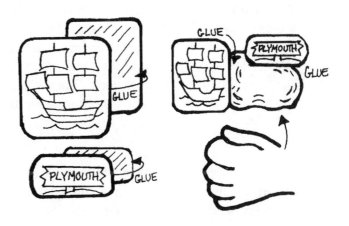

> **Materials:** one fist-sized rock for each child; crayons; scissors; glue; hot glue gun (optional); copies of page 87

> **Directions:** If possible, take students on a nature hike to look for fist-sized rocks. Otherwise, collect the rocks yourself. Tell the children to color and cut out the two copies of the *Mayflower* and the Plymouth sign. Have them glue the two copies back to back so that the ship and the sign can be viewed from either side. Then help them glue the *Mayflower* and Plymouth sign to their rocks. You may wish to use a hot glue gun to attach the pictures to the rock.

DAY 2

Sharing Time: Talk about how the Pilgrims lived in a new settlement. Tell how hard it was for them and how they had to do everything for themselves if they wanted to survive. Point out that they chopped down trees to build houses, made their own clothes, and prepared their own meals. Explain that they grew their own crops or hunted animals for food because there were no grocery stores back then. Draw a Venn diagram with the headings Us, Both, Pilgrims on the chalkboard. Encourage students to compare/contrast their lives with those of the Pilgrims. Allow students to refer to the books and pictures displayed on DAY 1 to get some ideas.

Lesson: Help with the Pies

> **Materials:** colored pencils or markers, copies of page 88

> **Directions:** First have the children count the number of cherries in each pie. Then have them trace the numbers on the pies in the boxes at the bottom of the page. Tell them to cut out these pies. Then ask them to glue each numbered pie onto the pie with the correct number of cherries.

Pilgrims *(cont.)*

DAY 3

Sharing Time: Continue talking about how the Native Americans helped the Pilgrims. Tell how they taught them to plant corn and save the seeds to plant again. Talk to them about giving thanks for things they have, food, clothes, and a home.

Arts and Crafts: Indian Corn Magnet

    Materials: white and green construction paper; glue; scissors; magnets; red, yellow, and orange tempera paint; aluminum pie tins; copies of page 89

    Directions: Cut pattern 1 (husk) out of green construction paper and pattern 2 (corn) out of white construction paper. Have the children glue pattern 2 behind pattern 1, making sure the top shows in the middle. Allow the glue to dry. Tell students that the kernels on Indian corn are different colors such as red, orange, and yellow. Show children how to make the kernels on the corn by dipping an index fingertip in some paint and printing it several times on the white construction paper. Add more paint, as needed. Then wipe your finger clean and do the same with a second color. Then follow the same procedure with the third color. Invite the children to follow your example.

DAY 4

Sharing Time: Talk about the Horn of Plenty and how it is always full of fruits and vegetables. Have the children tell what kind of fruit and vegetables they like to eat.

Arts and Crafts: Horn of Plenty Mobile

    Materials: watercolors, scissors, hole punch, yarn, copies of pages 90 and 91

    Directions: Have the children watercolor the horn of plenty and the fruits and vegetables. Next cut out all the pieces and punch a hole in each one. Using yarn, attach the pieces to make a horn of plenty mobile. Children may need help cutting out the pieces.

DAY 5

Cooking Experience: Pumpkin Pudding

    Materials: large bowl, measuring cups and spoons, large mixing spoon, small plastic bowls, plastic spoons, milk, can of pumpkin, one 3-ounce (75 g) package of vanilla pudding, honey, pumpkin spice

    Directions: In the large bowl, help the children mix 1½ cups (375 mL) of milk and the package of vanilla pudding. Add 1 cup (250 mL) canned pumpkin, ½ teaspoon (2.5 mL) pumpkin spice, and 1 tablespoon (15 mL) honey. Have the children take turns mixing the pudding until it is smooth. Then pour the pudding into a small bowl. Refrigerate for 15 minutes before serving it. This recipe makes 3 cups (750 mL) of pudding.

Name: _____ Date: _____

Plymouth Rock

Color and cut out both copies of the *Mayflower* and the Plymouth sign. Glue the two copies of the *Mayflower* back-to-back. Glue the two copies of the Plymouth sign back-to-back. Then glue the *Mayflower* and Plymouth sign onto the rock.

Name: _____ Date: _____

Help with the Pies

Count the number of cherries in each pie.

Trace the numbers on the pies in the boxes. Cut out these pies. Glue each numbered pie onto the pie with the correct number of cherries.

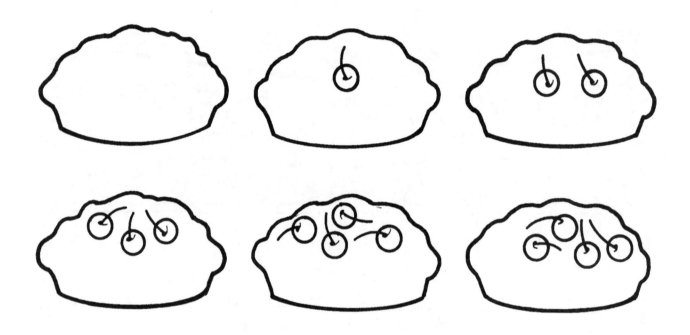

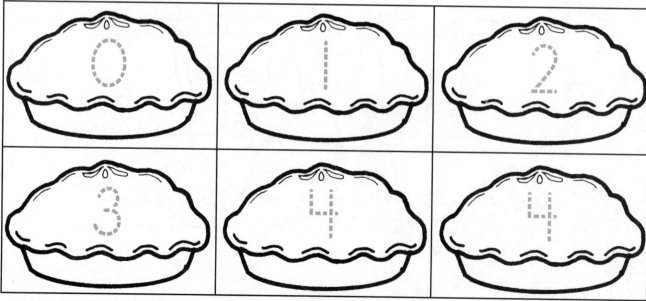

Name: _____   Date: _____

Indian Corn Magnet Pattern

Cut out the kernels pattern. Glue it behind the corn husk so that it shows.

Husk   **Kernels**

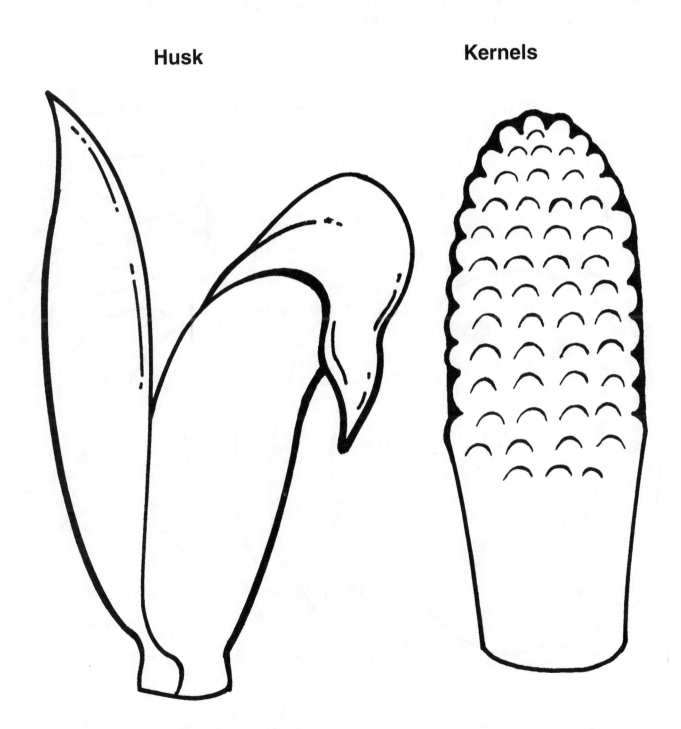

Horn of Plenty Mobile

Use watercolors to paint the horn of plenty below and the vegetables and fruits on page 91. Use a hole punch to make the holes where there are black dots. Cut six pieces of yarn that are different lengths. Tie the yarn to attach the vegetables and fruit to the horn of plenty. Then cut another piece of yarn. Tie it to the top of the horn of plenty. Hang the mobile from the ceiling.

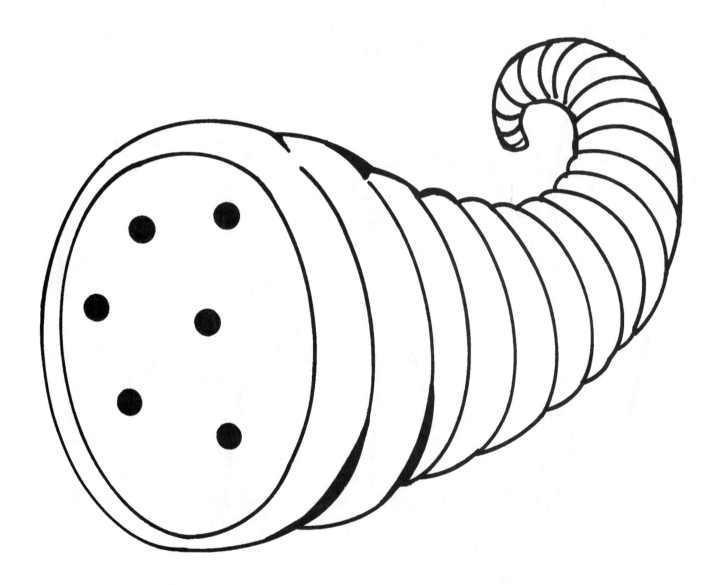

Horn of Plenty Mobile *(cont.)*

Thanksgiving and Turkeys

DAY 1

Sharing Time: Tell students that the Pilgrims and the Native Americans became friends. Explain that they taught each other different things. Then tell how the Pilgrims and Native Americans came together to celebrate the first Thanksgiving dinner. In addition, teach the class what a rectangle is. Have students brainstorm a list of objects in the classroom that have the rectangle shape.

Lesson: The First Thanksgiving

> **Materials:** crayons, copies of page 95

> **Directions:** Have the children examine the picture. Ask them to identify any objects in the picture that are rectangles. Examples: belt buckles, shoe buckles, hat buckles, table, table legs, and pieces of fringe on the Native American clothes. Have the children describe the things shown in the picture that the Pilgrims and Native Americans shared. Then have the children color the picture.

DAY 2

Sharing Time: Have the children talk about things for which they are thankful. Accept all responses. Examples: parents, family members, teachers, pets, food, clothes, toys, homes.

Lesson: I Am Thankful For...

> **Materials:** magazines, colored pencils, scissors and glue, copies of page 96

> **Directions:** Have the children brainstorm a list of things for which they are thankful. Write their suggestions on the chalkboard. Tell them to use the frame on page 96 to show some of the things for which they are thankful. They can either draw these things or cut out and glue pictures of them from magazines.

DAY 3

Sharing Time: Show pictures of turkeys and point out how they have different colored feathers. In addition, review the letters A-I and the colors brown, orange, yellow, red, and blue.

Movement Activity: Have students practice "The Turkey" (page 94) all week.

Lesson: Color the Turkey

> **Materials:** crayons or markers, copies of page 98

> **Directions:** Review the directions on page 98 with students. Make sure they understand that each letter represents one color. Explain that each time they see a particular letter on the turkey, they should color the feathers the designated color. Example: All the G's should be colored yellow. You may wish to color a turkey before the lesson so you can hang it up and let the children use it as a reference while they are coloring their turkeys.

Thanksgiving and Turkeys *(cont.)*

DAY 4

Sharing Time: Continue talking about turkeys. Discuss how big they are, what they look like, what noises they make, etc.

Game: Hide and Find the Turkeys

This game is played like hide-and-seek. One child pretends to be a farmer and counts aloud, while the other children pretend to be turkeys and hide. When the farmer finds the turkeys, they flap their arms like wings and say "gobble, gobble" as they race the farmer back to home base.

Lesson: Turkeys

> **Materials:** colored pencils or crayons, copies of page 97

> **Directions:** Have the children trace the numbers and also have them write some 4s of their own. Then have them color the turkeys.

DAY 5

Cooking Experience: Turkey Toast

> **Materials:** toaster; turkey-shaped cookie cutter; paper plates; plastic knives; wheat bread; creamy peanut butter; fruit-flavored, o-shaped cereal; tube of red gel icing

> **Directions:** Toast the bread. Dark brown toast works best. Then give each child a piece of toast. Let the children use the turkey cookie cutter to cut a turkey from the toast. Next have the children spread peanut butter on the back part of the turkey. Tell them to place the fruit-flavored, o-shaped cereal on top of the peanut butter to make the turkey's feathers. Show them how to use one piece of cereal with a little peanut butter on it to make an eye and red gel icing to make the turkey's wattle.

The Turkey

Movement Activity

The turkey is a funny bird.

His head goes wobble, wobble.

(Nod head up and down.)

All it says is just one word—

Gobble! Gobble! Gobble!

(Walk and gobble like a turkey.)

Traditional

Name: _____ Date: _____

The First Thanksgiving

This picture shows the Pilgrims and the Native Americans sharing the first Thanksgiving. Color the picture.

Name: _____ Date: _____

I Am Thankful For...

Think of things for which you are thankful. Draw some of these things or cut out pictures from magazines and glue them below.

Name: _____ Date: _____

Turkeys

Trace the numbers. Then color the turkeys.

Trace the 4s. Then write some by yourself.

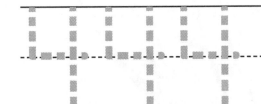

Name: _____   Date: _____

Color the Turkey

Color the **E**'s brown.

Color the **F**'s orange.

Color the **G**'s yellow.

Color the **H**'s red.

Color the **I**'s blue.

December

Sunday	Monday	Tuesday	Wednesday	Thursday	Friday	Saturday

Stars

=== **DAY 1** ===

Sharing Time: Start talking about stars and reviewing numbers 1–5. This week, tell the children that they are all shining stars because of something they are doing, like sharing toys, picking up and putting things away, etc.

Movement Activity: Have students practice the song "Twinkle, Twinkle, Little Star" (below) all week. While they sing the song, have them pretend to be looking up at a star in the night sky.

> **Twinkle, Twinkle, Little Star**
>
> Twinkle, twinkle, little star,
>
> How I wonder what you are.
>
> Up above the world so high,
>
> Like a diamond in the sky.
>
> Twinkle, twinkle, little star,
>
> How I wonder what you are!

Lesson: Bells and Stars

    Materials: crayons or colored pencils, copies of page 102

    Directions: Have the children trace the numbers 1–5. Then have them color the bells red and the stars yellow.

=== **DAY 2** ===

Sharing Time: Talk about stars and how bright they are and how people use them to decorate Christmas trees.

Lesson: Find the Stars

    Materials: markers, copies of page 103

    Directions: Have the children circle and color the stars in each row. In the boxes, they should write the number that shows how many stars are in each row.

=== **DAY 3** ===

Sharing Time: Continue talking about stars. Draw a five-pointed star on the chalkboard. Together, count the number of points that the star has. Write the number 5 on the chalkboard.

Lesson: Five Stars

    Materials: colored pencils, copies of page 104

    Directions: Have the children trace the 5s and write some by themselves. Next ask them to color 5 stars.

Stars (cont.)

DAY 4

Sharing Time: Talk about the similarities and differences among stars.

Arts and Crafts: Shining Star

> **Materials:** Option 1—watercolors, glitter, glue, scissors, copies of page 105
>
> Option 2—3" (7.5 cm) wooden stars, washable paint, paintbrushes, glue, glitter, ornament hangers
>
> **Directions:** Option 1—Have the children paint the star pattern (page 105) using watercolors. Then tell them to smear glue on the star and sprinkle glitter onto the glue. Allow the glue to dry and shake off any excess glitter. As an alternative to the child decorating with glitter, you may wish to write something special, such as "Joey is a star!" using a glitter glue pen. Then have the children cut out their stars. Display them in the classroom.
>
> Option 2—Provide students with wooden stars. Invite the children to paint their stars. Then have them smear glue on the stars and sprinkle glitter onto the glue. Allow the glue to dry and shake off any excess glitter. Put an ornament hanger through each star. Hang the stars as Christmas tree decorations.

DAY 5

Cooking Experience: Star Cookies

> **Materials:** cookie sheet, spray oil, spatula, star-shaped cookie cutter, rolling pin, cutting board, flour, pre-made sugar cookie dough, colored sugar, candy decorations
>
> **Directions:** Help the children roll out the cookie dough on a floured cutting board. Using a star-shaped cookie cutter, have each child cut out one or two cookies and place them on a sprayed cookie sheet. Allow the children to decorate their cookies with colored sugar or candies. Bake in the oven according to cookie dough package. Allow the cookies to cool before serving them to the children.

Game: Star Hunt

> **Directions:** Before students arrive, cut out several copies of the star pattern (page 105) from yellow poster board. Hide the stars around the classroom. When the children arrive, tell them that they are going to have a star hunt. Announce how many stars each student is allowed to find. Stress that they should not find more than the designated amount so that everyone has the opportunity to find the stars. Then allow time for them to hunt for the stars.

Name: _____ Date: _____

Bells and Stars

Trace the numbers. Color the bells red. Color the stars yellow.

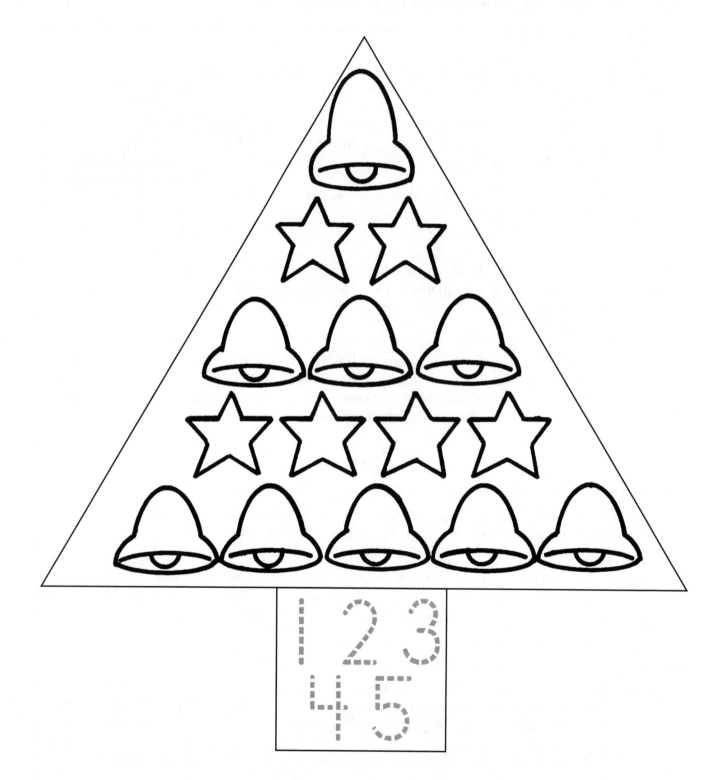

Name: _____ Date: _____

Find the Stars

Circle and color the stars in each row. In the boxes, write the number that shows how many stars are in each row.

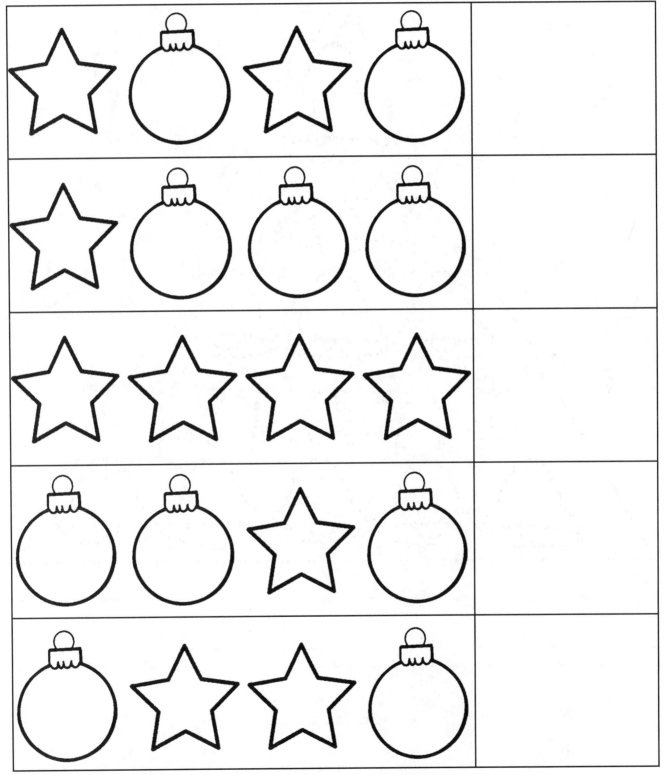

Name: _____   Date: _____

Five Stars

Color 5 of the stars.

Trace the 5s. Then write some by yourself.

Name: _____ Date: _____

Shining Star

Decorate the star, using tempera paint and glitter. Then cut out the star.

Hanukkah and Kwanzaa

Different holidays are celebrated by cultures around the world. Hanukkah and Kwanzaa are just two of these special occasions. You may wish to plan additional lessons to acquaint students with a variety of cultural holidays and celebrations throughout the year.

═══════════════════ **DAY 1** ═══════════════════

Sharing Time: Start this week by talking about the Jewish holiday Hanukkah, which is often called the Festival of Lights. Explain that it has been celebrated for 2000 years around the world. Coming in late fall or early winter, Jewish families honor Judah Maccabee's victory over King Antiochus, thus winning the right for his people to worship their own God. Miraculously, a one-day supply of oil burned for the full eight-day victory celebration. The lighting of the menorah candles, family feasts, dreidel games, latkes (potato pancakes) and applesauce, and gold-wrapped chocolate coins are all part of this special occasion.

Lesson: Festival of Lights

> **Materials:** crayons, scissors, glue, copies of page 108

> **Directions:** First have the children cut out the candles. Then ask them to match the uppercase letters on the menorah with the lowercase letters on the candles. Tell them to glue the candles in place above the matching uppercase letters. Encourage students to color the candles and menorah.

═══════════════════ **DAY 2** ═══════════════════

Sharing Time: Read aloud a book or story about Hanukkah. If possible, show students a dreidel, which is a spinning top.

Arts and Crafts: Dreidel

> **Materials:** sharpened pencils, 3" (7.5 cm) Styrofoam cubes, foil wrapping paper, cellophane tape, black permanent marker, tokens, cup

> **Directions:** Give each child a 3" (7.5 cm) Styrofoam cube and a piece of foil wrapping paper. Show students how to wrap the cube and tape the paper in place. Next take the sharpened pencil and push it through the 3" (7.5 cm) cube. From the chart shown below, write the Hebrew letters, one on each side of the cube. Help students make their dreidels. To play the game, give each player the same number of tokens. Have each player start the game by putting two tokens into cup. The players spin the top and can win or lose the tokens that are in the cup. Use the following chart to play the game.

נ	Nun	You win nothing.
ג	Gimel	You win all of the tokens in the cup.
ה	He	You take half the tokens in the cup.
ש	Shin	You must put one more token in the cup.

Hanukkah and Kwanzaa *(cont.)*

DAY 3

Sharing Time: Tell students the story behind the celebration of Kwanzaa. It is a holiday that was started in 1966 by an African-American professor named Maulana Ron Karenga. Kwanzaa means first for the African tribal celebration of the first harvest of crops each year. Observed from December 26 through January 1, Americans of African descent remember and honor their ancestors, their beliefs, and their family ties and traditions. Seven candles are lit on a kinara (candleholder), one each day for seven guiding principles, and the family talks about the special meaning of the day. Families and friends give small homemade gifts and enjoy special foods. The last day is filled with feasting and dancing.

Arts and Crafts: Kwanzaa Chains

    Materials: red, green, black construction paper; glue, scissors

    Directions: The children cut 1" x 6" (2.5 cm x 15 cm) strips of red, green, and black construction paper. Have them make paper chains with the strips of paper and glue. Help them decorate a tree or the classroom with the paper chains.

DAY 4

Sharing Time: Take students to the library. Allow students to look at books about Kwanzaa.

Arts and Crafts: Kwanzaa Candles

    Materials: birthday candles, seven per child; 2" x 6" x 2" (5 cm x 15 cm x 5 cm) Styrofoam rectangular prisms, one per child; foil wrapping paper; pencil; cellophane tape

    Directions: Show the children how to wrap the rectangular prism and tape the paper in place. Next demonstrate how to use the pencil point to poke seven small holes through the paper and into the Styrofoam. A candle should be able to fit in each hole. Insert seven candles into the holes. Warning: Do not light these candles.

DAY 5

Cooking Experience: Nutty Bananas

    Materials: bananas, one per child; 3 ounce (75 g) plastic cups; crushed nut topping, colored sugar, or other toppings (optional); wooden toothpicks; plastic knives; small paper plates

    Directions: Let the children peel their bananas. Next have them use the plastic knives to cut them into pieces. Be sure they cut the pieces on the paper plates. Then have them use a toothpick to pick up a piece of banana and dip it into the nuts or other toppings.

Name: _____ Date: _____

Festival of Lights

Cut out the candles and glue them in the right holder by matching the uppercase and lowercase letters. Then color the menorah and the candles.

Name: _____   Date: _____

Reindeer

=== **DAY 1** ===

Sharing Time: Engage the children in a discussion about reindeer. Tell about Rudolph.

Movement Activity: Have students learn the song "Rudolph the Red Nose Reindeer" all week. Allow them to make up movements to go with the song.

Lesson: Help Rudolph Find Santa

    Materials: crayons, copies of page 110

    Directions: Have the children draw a line from Rudolph to Santa. Point out that there is only one path that will lead Rudolph to Santa. Invite students to finish coloring the picture.

=== **DAY 2** ===

Sharing Time: Review the letters A–I and the colors red, green, pink, brown, and black. Before having students do the Rudolph activity, make a chart to show which color goes with each letter.

Lesson: Rudolph

    Materials: crayons, copies of page 111

    Directions: Have the children color the picture using the designated colors.

=== **DAY 3** ===

Sharing Time: Explain that Santa had 8 reindeer. Note: The number 8 is taught out of sequence because students will hear about Santa's 8 reindeer. You may wish to teach students the numbers 6, 7, and 8 before having them do the following lesson.

Lesson: Eight Reindeer

    Materials: crayons or colored pencils, copies of page 112

    Directions: Have the children trace the 8s and write some by themselves. Next have them color eight of the reindeer.

=== **DAY 4** ===

Sharing Time: Invite students to share experiences about things they have lost and later found.

Lesson: The Eight Lost Reindeer

    Materials: colored pencils, copies of page 113

    Directions: Have the children carefully examine the picture. Tell them to find and circle the eight hidden reindeer. Then encourage them to color the picture.

=== **DAY 5** ===

Cooking Experience: Peanut Butter Reindeer

    Materials: large bowl, wooden mixing spoon, wax paper, measuring cups and spoons, $\frac{1}{2}$ cup (125 mL) peanut butter, 2 tablespoons (30 mL) honey, 2 tablespoons (30 mL) sesame seeds, $\frac{1}{3}$ cup (83 mL) powdered milk, raisins, red hots, small pretzel knots broken to resemble antlers

    Directions: Use the spoon to mix the peanut butter, honey, sesame seeds, and powdered milk together in the large bowl. Give each child a piece of wax paper and a spoonful of the mixture. Let the children use their hands to shape the mixture into a reindeer's head. Use the broken pretzels for the antlers.

Name: _____ Date: _____

Help Rudolph Find Santa

Draw a line to show how Rudolph can get to Santa.

Name: _____ Date: _____

Rudolph

Use the letters to color the picture of Rudolph.

Color Key

A—red   D—brown

B—green   E—black

C—pink

Name: _____ Date: _____

Eight Reindeer

Color eight of the reindeer.

Trace the 8s. Then write some by yourself.

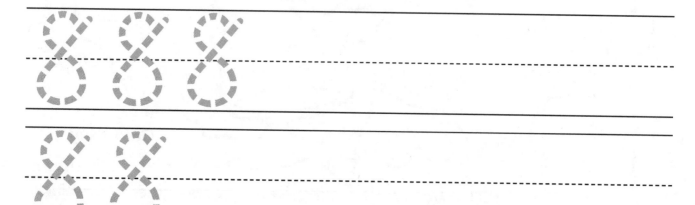

Name: _____ Date: _____

The Eight Lost Reindeer

Find and circle 8 reindeer. Then color the picture.

Gifts

DAY 1

Sharing Time: This week talk about gifts and sharing with others. Explain that it is better to give than to receive.

Lesson: Presents

> **Materials:** colored pencils or fine-point markers, copies of page 116
>
> **Directions:** Have the children trace the numbers and color the corresponding number of presents in each row.

DAY 2

Sharing Time: Invite students to brainstorm a list of presents that they would like to receive for Christmas. Write their ideas on the chalkboard. If you have students who do not celebrate this holiday, ask them to think of presents that they would like to receive for any occasion.

Lesson: I Wish For....

> **Materials:** toy catalogs, Christmas catalogs, or magazines with pictures of toys; crayons; scissors; glue; copies of page 117
>
> **Directions:** Explain to students that they are going to cut and glue pictures of things that they wish they could receive as presents. Stress that this does not mean that they will actually receive these gifts. To begin, have the children find pictures of things they would like to receive as gifts for Christmas in catalogs or magazines. These can include toys, clothes, and pets. Have them cut out the pictures and glue them onto the gift (page 117). If students cannot find pictures of the things they want, encourage them to draw these items. You may wish to share the completed projects with parents to give them some gift ideas.

DAY 3

Arts and Crafts: Have the children make one or more of the following gifts for their parents.

Candle Holder

> **Materials:** small baby food jars, one per child; red, green, and black permanent markers; votive candles; small felt circles, cut to fit the bottom of the baby food jars; tissue paper; curling ribbon; gift tags, glue, hot glue gun (optional)
>
> **Directions:** Give each child a baby food jar and one of each color marker. Have the children use the red and green markers to color the outside of the baby food jar. Allow the marker to dry. Then show the children how to use a black marker to draw lines so that the jar looks like a stained glass window. Help the children glue the felt onto the bottom of the jars using a hot glue gun. Place a votive candle inside each baby food jar. Help students wrap the jars for Christmas presents using tissue paper, curling ribbon, and gift tags.

Gifts *(cont.)*

=== **DAY 3** *(cont.)* ===

Plaster Handprint

Materials: plaster of Paris; water; wooden stirrer; disposable bowl; 8" (20 cm) aluminum pie pans, one per child; permanent marker; glitter, various colors; colored tissue paper; curling ribbon; gift tags

Directions: In the bowl, mix up the plaster of Paris according to the directions on the package. Write a child's name or initials on each pie pan. Pour 1" (2.5 cm) of wet plaster into the pie pans. Then help each child make a handprint by spreading his/her fingers apart, pressing the hand into the wet plaster, and carefully pulling the hand back out. While the plaster is still wet, sprinkle glitter around the handprint, making sure not to get any on the handprint itself. Allow the plaster to dry overnight. Gently peel off the pie pan and remove the plaster handprint. Help the children wrap their handprints with the tissue paper, curling ribbon, and gift tags.

Christmas Tree Magnet

Materials: pre-cut green felt Christmas trees, picture of each child, glitter, sequins, glue, magnets, hot glue gun, tissue paper, curling ribbon, gift tags

Directions: To prepare for this activity, take close-up individual photographs of the children and cut out a green felt Christmas tree for each child. Cut a circle around the child's face in each photograph. Tell the children to glue their photographs onto the Christmas trees. Let the children use sequins and glitter to decorate their trees. Then use a hot glue gun to attach two small magnets to the back of each Christmas tree. Allow the glue to dry. Then ask the children to wrap their trees with tissue paper, curling ribbon, and gift tags.

=== **DAY 4** ===

Sharing Time: Have a Christmas party and gift/book exchange. These can be done on any day of the week. They can be combined with other activities or done on a separate day as they are described here. Decide ahead of time, what kind of a party you want. (Examples: pizza, fruit and vegetable, cookies and punch) Before the day of the party, decide if you want the children to have a gift exchange or book exchange. Then be sure to give parents plenty of notice about what the children should bring. On the day of the party, play Christmas music, games, or videos.

=== **DAY 5** ===

Cooking Experience: Surprise Pudding

Materials: large bowl, whisk, measuring cup, plastic cups, plastic spoons, instant vanilla pudding, milk, small unwrapped Christmas candies

Directions: Help the children make the pudding according to the directions on the package. Pour the pudding into plastic cups. When the children aren't watching, push the Christmas candies into the pudding. Refrigerate for 15 minutes. Serve the pudding. While the children are eating it, they will discover the surprise candies inside.

Name: _____ Date: _____

Presents

Trace the numbers. Color the correct number of presents in each row.

Color **1** present.

Color **2** presents.

Color **3** presents.

Color **4** presents.

Color **5** presents.

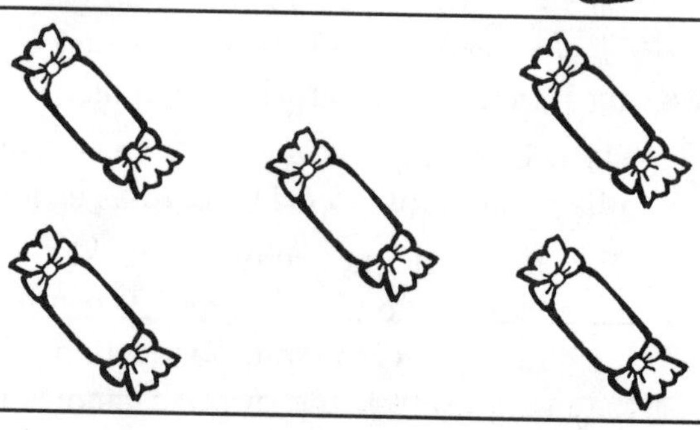

Name: _____ Date: _____

I Wish For....

Think about things that you would like to get for Christmas. Find pictures of these things in magazines and catalogs. Cut out and glue the pictures onto the present shown below.

January

Sunday	Monday	Tuesday	Wednesday	Thursday	Friday	Saturday

Hot and Cold Weather

DAY 1

Sharing Time: Compare/contrast hot and cold weather. Talk about how cold weather affects people, animals, and plants. Ask students to name things that are hot and others that are cold.

Movement Activity: Have students practice "The Sounds of Winter" (page 120) all week.

Lesson: Hot and Cold

   Materials: red and blue crayons or markers, copies of page 121

   Directions: Have students use blue crayons or markers to color the pictures of things that are cold. Then have them use red crayons or markers to color the pictures of things that are hot.

DAY 2

Sharing Time: Have children talk about types of weather. Invite volunteers to tell what type of weather is their favorite and explain why.

Arts and Crafts: Favorite Weather

   Materials: blank paper and colored pencils

   Directions: Have students draw pictures of themselves enjoying their favorite kind of weather. Ask them to dictate a sentence about their scenes as you write it on their papers.

DAY 3

Sharing Time: Review the different kinds of weather. Tell students what a meteorologist does.

Lesson: Weather Wheel

   Materials: scissors, brads, crayons, copies of pages 122 and 123

   Directions: Have students color the top wheel and the pictures on the bottom wheel. Tell them to cut out both wheels. Help them cut out the wedge with the dotted lines from the top wheel. Show them how to place the top wheel on the bottom wheel with the edges aligned and the colored sides up. Have students push a brad through the centers of both wheels. Each day ask them to turn the top wheel until the window shows a picture of what the weather is like.

DAY 4

Arts and Crafts: Weather Scene

   Materials: scissors, glue, construction paper, crayons, markers, colored pencils, sequins, cotton balls, felt, sand, crushed Styrofoam, tissue paper, etc.

   Directions: Invite the children to make a weather scene.

DAY 5

Cooking Experience: Hot and Cold Gelatin

   Materials: pan; mixing bowl; measuring cup; spoon; ice cubes; water; package of gelatin; individual cups, one per child; plastic spoons, one per child

   Directions: While making the gelatin, talk about how the boiling water is hot and the ice cubes are cold. After the gelatin has been made, pour it into individual cups and put them in the refrigerator.

The Sounds of Winter

Movement Activity

Listen with your ears. Do you hear winter?

(Cup one ear with a hand and listen.)

The wind goes whooo, whooo, whooo!

(Make the wind sound.)

Look with your eyes. Do you see winter?

(Open eyes wide and look all around.)

The snowflakes are falling slowly.

(Raise arms. Slowly glide hands from right to left while lowering arms.)

Listen with your ears. Do you hear winter?

(Cup one ear with a hand and listen.)

The rain goes plip, plop. The thunder goes bang!

(Raise arms. Wiggle fingers while lowering arms. Clap hands for thunder.)

Look with your eyes. Do you see winter?

(Open eyes wide and look all around.)

The sun is shining large and bright.

(Smile. Put hands above head and form circle with arms.)

Deanna Reynolds

Name: _____ Date: _____

Hot and Cold

Circle the **cold** things blue. Circle the **hot** things red. Then color the pictures.

Name: _____ Date: _____

Weather Wheel

Color and cut out top wheel shown below. Cut out the wedge with the dotted lines. Color the pictures on page 123. Cut out the bottom wheel. Place the top wheel on the bottom wheel with the colored sides up. Push a brad through the centers of both wheels to hold the wheels together. Each day turn the top wheel to show the picture of what your weather is like.

Top Wheel

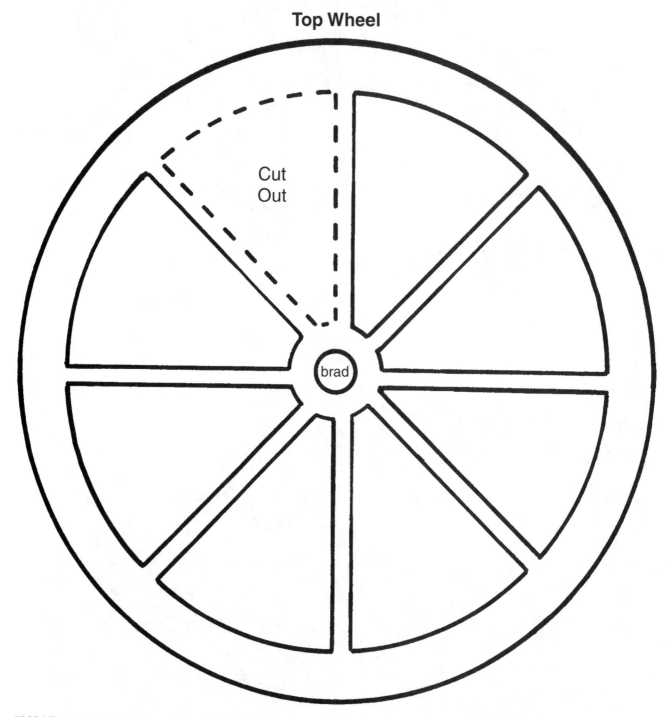

Name: _____ Date: _____

Weather Wheel *(cont.)*

Bottom Wheel

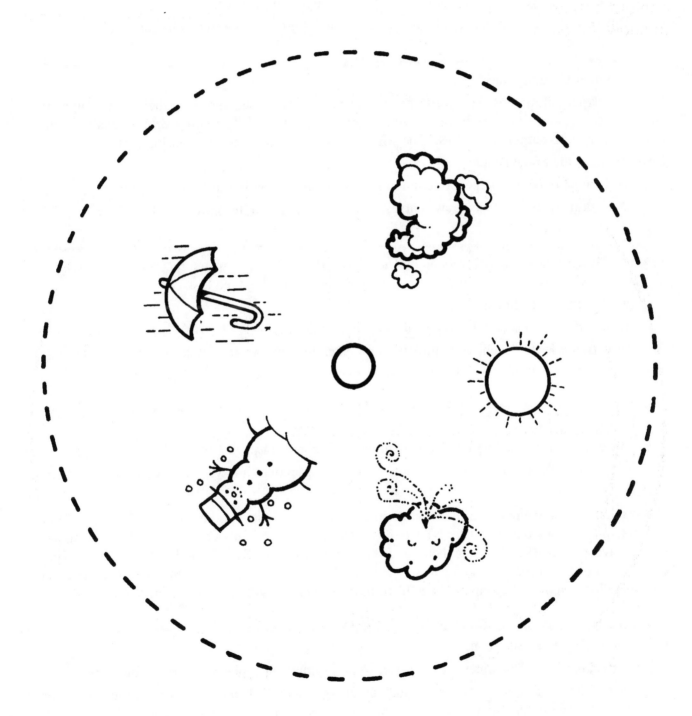

Winter Clothing

═══════════════ **DAY 1** ═══════════════

Sharing Time: Talk about cold weather and how to dress for cold winters.

Lesson: What Would You Wear?

   Materials: crayons, markers or colored pencils, copies of page 125

   Directions: Have students circle the pieces of clothing that they might wear on a cold day.

═══════════════ **DAY 2** ═══════════════

Game: Winter Clothing Race

Provide a variety of mittens, hats, earmuffs, and scarves, or have students bring their own. Divide the class into two teams. Place each team's winter clothing in a pile. When you give the signal to begin, both teams race to put on the clothes. The winner is the team that finishes dressing first.

Lesson: Dress the Snow People

   Materials: crayons, markers or colored pencils, copies of page 126

   Directions: Have students draw scarves, hats, and mittens on the snow people.

═══════════════ **DAY 3** ═══════════════

Sharing Time: Read aloud any version of *The Three Little Kittens*, or play a recording of it. Explain that if the kittens had put away their mittens, they would not have gotten lost.

Lesson: Kittens' Lost Mittens

   Materials: crayons or colored pencils, copies of page 127

   Directions: Have the children draw lines to match the mitten pairs. Ask them to color the mittens, making sure the pairs are colored the same.

═══════════════ **DAY 4** ═══════════════

Lesson: Finding Mittens

   Materials: brown and yellow markers or crayons, copies of page 128

   Directions: Have students use brown to color the big mittens and yellow to color the small ones.

Game: Pass the Mitten

Have students sit in a circle. Place one child in the center. Ask that child to close his/her eyes. While you play music from a tape or record, have the children in the circle pass a mitten. When you stop the music, have everyone quickly hide their hands behind their backs. Say, "Who has the mitten?" The center child opens his/her eyes and guesses who has the mitten. After finding the mitten, the two players trade places. Give everyone a chance to be in the center of the circle.

═══════════════ **DAY 5** ═══════════════

Cooking Experience: Snowcones

   Materials: ice cubes, water, frozen juice, blender, small cups, plastic spoons, tablespoon

   Directions: Thaw the juice. Crush small amounts of ice in a blender. Add water until you have a thick snowy mixture. Pour the mixture into the cups and drizzle 2-3 tablespoons (30-45 mL) of juice over the "snow."

Name: _____ Date: _____

What Would You Wear?

Circle the pieces of clothing that you might wear on a cold day.

Name: _____ Date: _____

Dress the Snow People

Each snow person needs to be dressed for the cold winter day. Draw a scarf, hat, and mittens on each snow person.

Name: _____ Date: _____

Kittens' Lost Mittens

The kittens have mixed up their mittens! Draw lines to match the pairs of mittens. Then color the matching pairs using the same colors.

Name: _____ Date: _____

Finding Mittens

Find the **big** mittens. Color the big mittens brown.

Find the **small** mittens. Color the small mittens yellow.

Snowflakes

═══════════════════════════ **DAY 1** ═══════════════════════════

Sharing Time: Talk about snowflakes. Point out that no two snowflakes are alike.

Movement Activity: Have students practice "Snowflakes" (page 130) all week.

Lesson: Matching Snowflakes

> **Materials:** colored pencils or markers, copies of page 131

> **Directions:** Have children draw lines to pair the snowflakes that match in size.

═══════════════════════════ **DAY 2** ═══════════════════════════

Lesson: Seven Snowflakes

> **Materials:** colored pencils, copies of page 132

> **Directions:** Have children color 7 snowflakes. Then have them trace and write the number 7.

═══════════════════════════ **DAY 3** ═══════════════════════════

Sharing Time: Read aloud *The Snowy Day* by Ezra Jack Keats (Viking, 1962).

Lesson: Coloring Snowflakes

> **Materials:** colored pencils, copies of page 133

> **Directions:** Have the children color the designated number of snowflakes in each box. Then have them trace the numbers 5, 6, and 7.

═══════════════════════════ **DAY 4** ═══════════════════════════

Arts and Crafts: Snowflake Mobile

> **Materials:** 4" x 18" (10 cm x 46 cm) strips of blue poster board; scissors; hole punch; stapler; glue; glitter; pieces of yarn, nine for each child; copies of page 134

> **Directions:** Before students arrive, make the mobile frames by cutting strips of poster board; stapling the ends of each strip together to form a circle; and punching six holes in each strip, making sure the holes are about the same distance apart. When the children arrive, ask them to smear glue on the snowflakes and sprinkle glitter on the glue. Allow the glue to dry before shaking off any excess glitter. Then punch a hole in each snowflake. Help the children string a piece of yarn through each snowflake hole. Then tie the pieces of yarn to the mobile frame. At the top of each frame, punch three more holes, making sure they are about the same distance apart. Tie yarn to these holes. Use the yarn to hang the mobiles.

═══════════════════════════ **DAY 5** ═══════════════════════════

Cooking Experience: Sugar Snowflakes

> **Materials:** skillet, tongs, oil, flour tortillas, powdered sugar, plate

> **Directions:** Pour oil in a skillet until it is 1" (2.5 cm) deep. Heat the oil. Have students tear holes in tortillas so they look like snowflakes. Let the children watch from a safe distance as you fry the tortilla in the oil. Place the fried tortilla on a plate of powdered sugar. Turn the tortilla over to sugar the other side. Allow the Sugar Snowflakes to cool before allowing the children to eat them.

Snowflakes

Movement Activity

Snowflakes are falling without a sound.

(Raise arms. Wiggle fingers while moving arms down.)

Snowflakes are drifting to the ground.

(Move hands from side to side.)

Snowflakes are prancing like sheep.

(Prance fingers all around.)

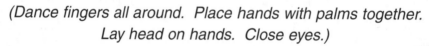

Snowflakes are dancing and then they fall asleep.

*(Dance fingers all around. Place hands with palms together.
Lay head on hands. Close eyes.)*

Deanna Reynolds

Name: _____ Date: _____

Matching Snowflakes

Look at the snowflakes. Two are small, two are medium, and two are large. Draw lines to match the snowflakes that are the same size.

Name: _____ Date: _____

Seven Snowflakes

Color 7 snowflakes.

Trace the 7s. Then write some by yourself.

Name: _____   Date: _____

Coloring Snowflakes

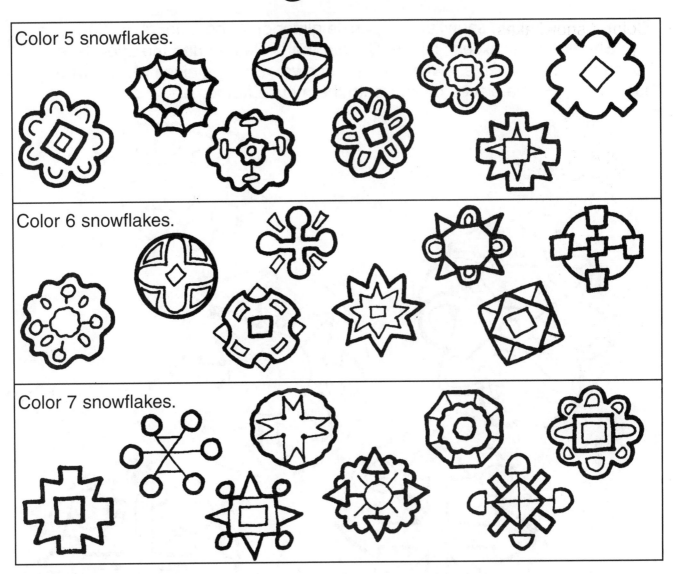

Color 5 snowflakes.

Color 6 snowflakes.

Color 7 snowflakes.

Now trace the numbers.

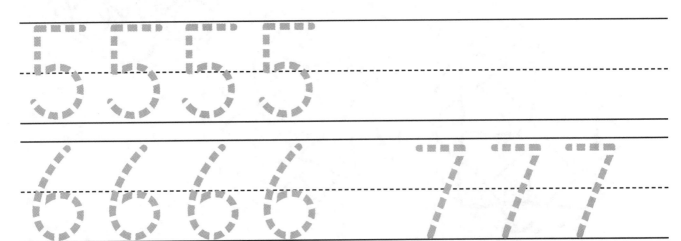

Name: _____ Date: _____

Snowflake Mobile

Smear glue on each snowflake. Sprinkle glitter onto the glue. Allow the glue to dry. Shake off any excess glitter. Cut out the circles around the snowflakes. Punch a hole on each snowflake where shown. String a piece of yarn through each hole. Tie the pieces of yarn onto the mobile frame.

Snow People

=== **DAY 1** ===

Sharing Time: Talk about winter weather. Ask the children what kinds of things they like to do in the snow. Answers might include throwing snowballs, building snow people, and making snow angels. If you do not live in an area where it snows, ask the children what kinds of things they would like to do if it snowed in your community.

Arts and Crafts: Winter Snow Person

> **Materials:** blue construction paper, crayons, glue, scissors, cotton balls, glitter, copies of page 137

> **Directions:** Ask students to color the snow person's eyes, nose, mouth, hat, and buttons. Have them cut out the four pieces — the three circles and the hat. Show them how to make the snow person by gluing the four pieces onto a sheet of blue construction paper. Allow students to glue cotton balls along the bottom of the construction paper to make it look like snow on the ground. Then have them make falling snowflakes by smearing glue on the construction paper and sprinkling silver glitter onto the glue. Allow the glue to dry before shaking off any excess glitter.

=== **DAY 2** ===

Sharing Time: If possible, build a snow person outside. If it is not possible, build one inside using white cotton balls.

Lesson: Object Hunt

> **Materials:** markers or colored pencils, copies of page 138

> **Directions:** Have the children look for the objects shown at the top of the page in the picture at the bottom of the page. Tell them to circle the ones they find.

=== **DAY 3** ===

Arts and Crafts: Winter Scene

> **Materials:** construction paper, cotton balls, Styrofoam pieces, glitter, glue, scissors, sequins, ribbons, etc.

> **Directions:** Have the children create their favorite winter scene with a snow person in it.

Game: Pass the Snowball

Have students pretend that a large white pom pom or a cotton ball is a snowball. Then have them sit in a circle. Place one child in the center. Ask that child to close her/his eyes. While you play music from a tape or record, have the children in the circle pass the snowball. When you stop the music, have everyone quickly hide their hands behind their backs. Say, "Who has the snowball?" The center child opens her/his eyes and guesses who has the snowflake. After finding the snowball, the two players trade places. Give everyone a chance to be in the center of the circle.

Snow People *(cont.)*

═══════════════════════════ **DAY 4** ═══════════════════════════

Sharing Time: Review with the children that winter is a time of cold weather. Take a winter walk around the school or to a nearby park. Be sure to check your school's policy about taking the children off campus before leaving the school grounds. While on the walk, have the children look for changes that have occurred due to the arrival of winter.

Lesson: Snow Person Search

   Materials: crayons or markers, copies of page 139

   Directions: Have the children use red to color the snow person with 3 buttons, use green to color the snow person wearing a scarf, use yellow to color the snow person with 2 pockets, use blue to color the snow person holding a broom.

═══════════════════════════ **DAY 5** ═══════════════════════════

Cooking Experience: Marshmallow Snow People

   Materials: toothpicks, craft sticks, large marshmallows, chocolate syrup, paper plates

   Directions: To make the snow people, give each child 2-3 large marshmallows. Show them how to push the marshmallows onto a craft stick. Then demonstrate how to draw facial features and clothing on the snow person by painting chocolate syrup on the marshmallows using the toothpicks. Pour a small amount of syrup onto the plate. Allow the children to dip the top of their snow people's heads in the syrup. Point out that this will make the snow people look like they are wearing hats.

Name: _____ Date: _____

Winter Snow Person

Color the snow person's eyes, nose, mouth, hat, and buttons. Cut out the four pieces—the three circles and the hat. Make the snow person by gluing the pieces onto a sheet of blue construction paper. Glue cotton balls along the bottom of the construction paper to make it look like snow on the ground. To make snowflakes falling from the sky, smear glue on the construction paper and sprinkle silver glitter onto the glue. Allow the glue to dry. Then shake off any extra glitter.

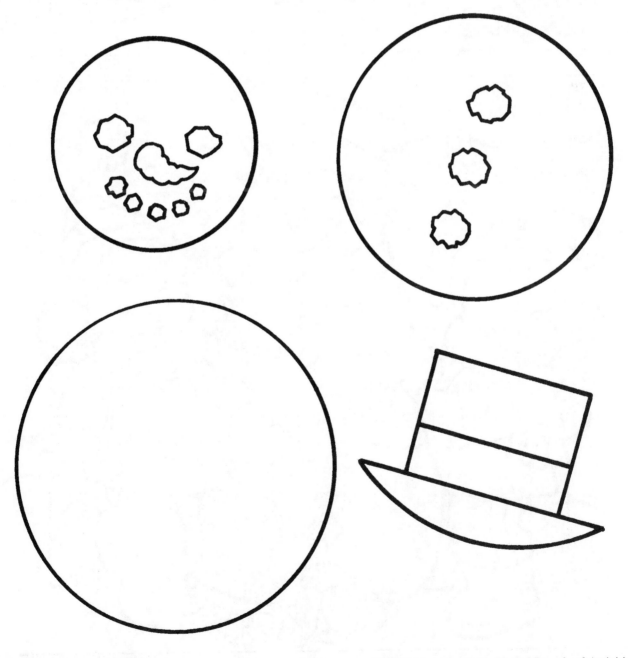

Name: _____ Date: _____

Object Hunt

Look for these objects in the picture below. Circle the ones you find.

Name: _____ Date: _____

Snow Person Search

1. Find the snow person with 3 buttons. Color it red.

2. Find the snow person wearing a scarf. Color it green.

3. Find the snow person with only 2 pockets. Color it yellow.

4. Find the snow person holding a broom. Color it blue.

Name: _____ Date: _____

Inuit

DAY 1

Sharing Time: Start talking about Inuit, snow, igloos, and Alaska.

Lesson: On the Ice

    Materials: crayons, colored pencils or markers, copies of page 141

    Directions: Have the children trace the object on the ice to find out what it is. Point out that today many Inuit live in homes like theirs but an igloo is a traditional type of shelter.

DAY 2

Sharing Time: Provide books and pictures of "Inuit" for the children to view.

Lesson: Finish Drawing the Igloo

    Materials: crayons, colored pencils or markers, copies of page 142

    Directions: Children need to finish drawing the igloo and then color the picture.

DAY 3

Sharing Time: Review the letters A-K. Introduce the letters M, N, and O.

Lesson: Igloo Letters

    Materials: colored pencils, copies of page 143

    Directions: Have the children draw lines to match the uppercase and lowercase letters. Then have them trace and write the letters M, N, and O.

DAY 4

Sharing Time: Bring one or more large furniture boxes. Paint the outside of each box white. Allow the paint to dry. Use black paint to draw lines for a snow block pattern on the white boxes. Have the children pretend they are Inuit living in igloos.

DAY 5

Cooking Experience: Edible Igloos

    Materials: small paper plates, plastic knives, ½ cored apple per child, peanut butter, mini-marsh-mallows

    Directions: Put ½ apple on each plate with the skin side up. Have the children spread peanut butter all over the skin of the apple. Tell them to stick mini-marshmallows onto the peanut butter until it is covered. Allow students to eat their igloos.

Name: _____ Date: _____

On the Ice

These Inuit see something on the ice. Trace the dotted lines to find out what they see.

Name: _____ Date: _____

Inuit

Inuit have black hair and brown skin. Traditionally they eat raw meat and fish. Inuit dress in warm clothes. Many Inuit travel on sleds pulled by dogs. Sometimes Inuit live in igloos made from blocks of frozen snow. Finish drawing the igloo with blocks of frozen snow. Then color the picture.

Name: _____ Date: _____

Igloo Letters

Draw lines to match the uppercase and lowercase letters.

E	g
F	e
G	f
H	m
I	k
J	l
K	j
L	n
M	h
N	i
O	o

Trace the letters. Then write some by yourself.

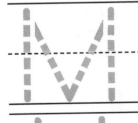

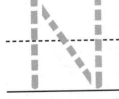

February

Sunday	Monday	Tuesday	Wednesday	Thursday	Friday	Saturday

Groundhog Day and Shadows

DAY 1

Sharing Time: Talk about how shadows are made when an object blocks light. Tell students the legend behind Groundhog Day. Allow students to make shadow puppets on the wall using their hands and a light source, such as a flashlight or overhead projector.

Lesson: Groundhog Sizes

> **Materials:** red, green, blue, and yellow crayons or markers; copies of page 146

> **Directions:** Have the children color the small groundhog red, the medium groundhog green, and the large groundhog blue. Tell them to trace and color the sun yellow.

DAY 2

Sharing Time: Have the children share personal experiences related to shadows.

Lesson: Animal Shadows

> **Materials:** markers or colored pencils, copies of page 147

> **Directions:** Ask the children to draw lines to match each animal to its shadow.

DAY 3

Games:

Groundhog Shadow Tag: Have one child be a groundhog. Have that child try to step on the other children's shadows. When the groundhog steps on a shadow, the child's whose shadow it is becomes the new groundhog. Continue the game until every child has been the groundhog.

Groundhog Hide-and-Seek: Let one child be "it," and have the others pretend to be groundhogs. Tell the child who is "it" to hide her/his eyes. Help that child count while the other children hide in their "burrows." Then have the child who is "it" try to find as many groundhogs as she/he can. Be sure every child has a turn being it.

DAY 4

Lesson: Groundhog Day

> **Materials:** crayons, markers, or colored pencils; copies of page 148

> **Directions:** Explain to the class that when the sun is shining, the groundhog will see its shadow. Have the children add to the picture by drawing the sun and the groundhog's shadow.

DAY 5

Cooking Experience: Groundhog in a Blanket

> **Materials:** can of biscuits, package of hot dogs, cheese slices (optional), cookie sheet, spray oil

> **Directions:** Cut each hot dog into three pieces. If desired, cut each slice of cheese into two triangles. Have students stretch the biscuits to make the "blankets." Tell them to hide a piece of hot dog and cheese inside their biscuits. Have them pretend that the hot dog is the groundhog. Place the groundhogs in the blankets on a cookie sheet covered with spray oil. Bake them at 350 degrees Fahrenheit (175 degrees Celsius) for 12 minutes. After baking, invite students to see which groundhogs peeked out to see their shadows and which ones didn't. Cool before serving.

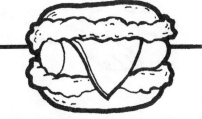

Name: _____ Date: _____

Groundhog Sizes

Color the small groundhog red, the medium groundhog green, and the large groundhog blue. Trace and color the sun yellow.

Name: _____ Date: _____

Animal Shadows

Draw lines to match each animal to its shadow.

Name: _____ Date: _____

Groundhog Day

When the sun is shining, the groundhog will see its shadow. Draw the sun and the groundhog's shadow.

Post Office and Addresses

DAY 1

Sharing Time: Talk about how important it is for students to learn their addresses. Explain how the post office processes the mail and the mail carriers deliver it. If possible, take a field trip to a post office or have a postal employee speak to your class. Allow time for the children to practice reciting their addresses until they are memorized. Some children may need additional practice.

Lesson: Mailbox and Family

   Materials: watercolors, paintbrushes, plastic cups, water, colored pencils, scissors, copies of page 150

   Directions: After reproducing the mailboxes, fill one out for each child. Then have the children paint their mailboxes with watercolors. Allow the paint to dry. Then tell the children to cut out the mailboxes. Have them draw themselves and their families on the back of their papers.

DAY 2

Lesson: The Postal Service

   Materials: crayons, colored pencils or markers, copies of page 151

   Directions: Tell students to draw lines to match the uppercase and lowercase letters.

DAY 3

Sharing Time: Tell students that the post office will not deliver mail unless it has stamps on it. If possible, show the class different kinds of stamps.

Lesson: Matching Letters and Stamps

   Materials: crayons or colored pencils, copies of page 152

   Directions: Have the children draw a line to connect each letter with its matching stamp. You may wish to have the children color the envelopes and stamps.

DAY 4

Lesson: Letters to Mail

   Materials: crayons, markers, or colored pencils, scissors and glue, copies of page 153

   Directions: Point out the letters at the bottom of the page. Help students notice that some are large and others are small. Tell students to color the large letters blue and the small ones red. Have them cut out all of the letters. Then have them glue the large letters under the large mailbox and the small letters under the small mailbox.

DAY 5

Cooking Experience: Letters and Envelopes

   Materials: plastic knives, paper plates, slices of cheese, small flour tortillas

   Directions: Have the children cut the tortillas into rectangles. Tell them to put a slice of cheese on one side and fold the tortilla rectangle in half. Bake the tortilla envelopes in a microwave for about 30 seconds or until the cheese melts. Allow these to cool before serving.

Name: _____ Date: _____

Mailbox and Family

Reproduce the mailbox. Print each child's name and address on a mailbox. Allow the children to paint their mailboxes with watercolors. Have them cut out their mailboxes. Then encourage them to draw a picture of themselves and their families on the other side of their mailboxes.

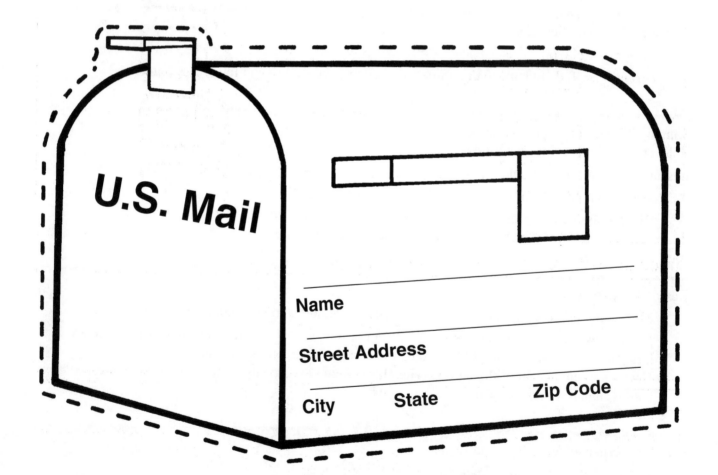

Name: _____ Date: _____

The Postal Service

Draw lines to match the uppercase and lowercase letters.

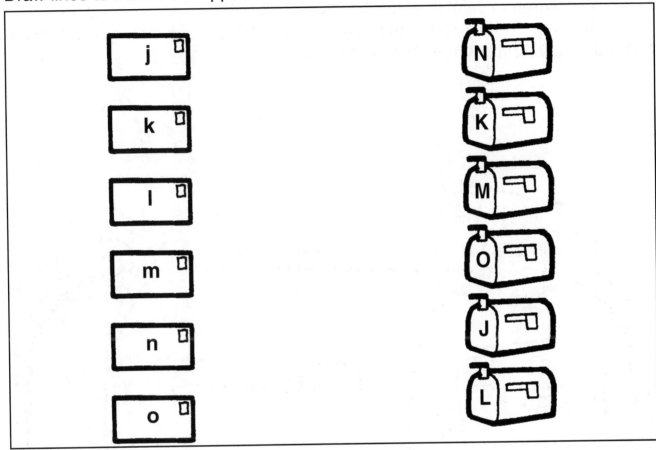

Trace the letters. Then write some by yourself.

Name: _____ Date: _____

Matching Letters and Stamps

Draw a line to connect each letter with its matching stamp.

Name: _____ Date: _____

Letters to Mail

Look at the letters at the bottom of the page. Some are large, and some are small. Color the large letters blue. Color the small letters red. Cut out all of the letters. Glue the large letters under the large mailbox. Glue the small letters under the small mailbox.

Valentine's Day

The lesson plan suggested below and on page 155 is organized with Valentine's Day falling on Thursday. Arrange this week's activities around the day on which February 14th falls. If this holiday occurs on a weekend, plan to do the DAY 4 activities on the preceding Friday.

DAY 1

Sharing Time: Talk about how Valentine's Day is a time to show others that you care about them. Have a discussion about feelings and how they are expressed appropriately. Invite students to brainstorm a list of emotions, such as sad, mad, scared, and happy. Then read aloud the following poem.

The Queen of Hearts

The Queen of Hearts
She made some tarts
All on a summer's day.
The Knave of Hearts
He stole the tarts
And took them clean away.

The King of Hearts
Called for the tarts
And beat the Knave full sore.
The Knave of Hearts
Brought back the tarts
And vowed he'd steal no more.

Traditional

Movement Activity: Have students practice "Valentine's Day" (page 156) all week.

Lesson: Happy and Sad Faces

Materials: crayons or colored pencils, copies of page 157

Directions: Have the children draw themselves with happy faces and tell what makes them happy. Then have the children draw themselves with sad faces and tell what makes them sad. Write the children's responses on the appropriate lines.

Valentine's Day *(cont.)*

═══════════════════════════ **DAY 2** ═══════════════════════════

Sharing Time: Talk to the children about the tradition of exchanging Valentine's Day cards.

Arts and Crafts: Valentine's Holder

> **Materials:** construction paper, various colors and sizes; paper plates; hole punch; shoe boxes; glitter; glue; scissors; decorative stickers, such as hearts and flowers; markers; crayons; yarn; other craft materials that are available.
>
> **Directions:** Have students make one of the following types of holders. (1) Hold two paper plates with the front sides together. Punch holes ⅔ of the way around, spacing them about an inch apart. Lace yarn through the holes. Tie the ends of the yarn above the open section of the plates to hang it up after it is decorated. (2) Cover a shoe box with tissue paper or construction paper. Then decorate it. Cut a slit in the top of the box so the Valentines can be placed in the box. (3) Fold an extra large sheet of construction paper in half. Glue the sides together, leaving the top open. Then decorate the envelope.

═══════════════════════════ **DAY 3** ═══════════════════════════

Lesson: The Queen of Hearts

> **Materials:** markers or colored pencils, copies of page 158
>
> **Directions:** Have the children trace the first heart, draw a sad face on it, and color it blue. Next have them trace the second heart, draw a happy face, and color it red.

═══════════════════════════ **DAY 4** ═══════════════════════════

Sharing Time: Valentine's Day Party

This is a day filled with fun activities, games, and delicious snacks. Decide what types of food, you want to serve. These might include sandwiches, chips and dip, or cookies and punch. During the party, allow time for the children to deliver their Valentines to each other.

Game: Pin the Nose on the Valentine's Face

Cut out a large, red, poster-board heart. Use black marker to draw a happy face on it without a nose. Cut out little construction paper hearts for the noses. Write a number on each heart. There should be one numbered heart for each child. To begin, place a piece of double-stick tape on the back of the numbered hearts. Blindfold the child with heart number 1. Spin that child around and have him/her try to stick the heart nose on the Valentine's face. Play until each child has had a turn. If some children do not want to wear a blindfold, just let them close their eyes.

═══════════════════════════ **DAY 5** ═══════════════════════════

Cooking Experience: Queen of Hearts Tarts

> **Materials:** can of biscuits, jar of strawberry preserves, plastic spoons, paper plates, cookie sheet, spray oil
>
> **Directions:** Have the children shape their biscuits into little bowls. Place the biscuits on the sprayed cookie sheet. Help each child put a spoonful of the preserves in the biscuit bowl. Bake in an oven at 350 degrees Fahrenheit (175 degrees Celsius) until the bottom of the biscuits are golden brown. Allow the biscuits to cool before serving them.

Valentine's Day

Movement Activity

Pink, purple, white, and blue.

(Form a heart shape with the index fingers and thumbs.)

I'll find a pretty one

(Pretend to be looking through a stack of Valentine's cards.)

And give it to you.

(Pretend to give a Valentine's card to someone.)

Deanna Reynolds

Name: _____ Date: _____

Happy and Sad Faces

Draw a happy face. Tell what makes you happy.
Then draw a sad face. Tell what makes you sad.

Happy

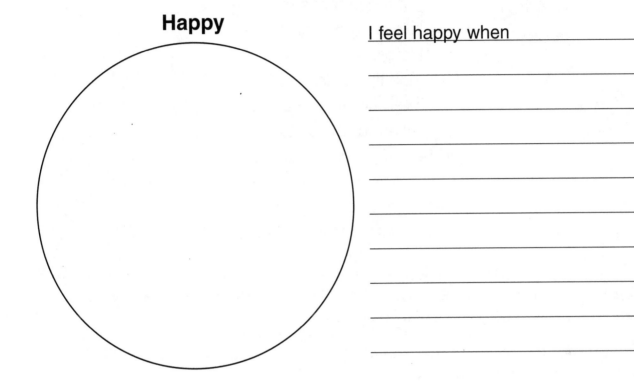

I feel happy when _____

_____

_____

_____

_____

_____

_____

_____

_____

_____

I feel sad when _____

_____

_____

_____

_____

_____

_____

_____

Sad

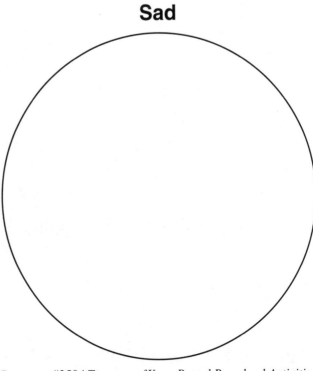

Name: _____ Date: _____

The Queen of Hearts

The Queen of Hearts
She made some tarts
All on a summer's day.
The Knave of Hearts
He stole the tarts
And took them clean away.
The King of Hearts
Called for the tarts
And beat the Knave full sore.
The Knave of Hearts
Brought back the tarts
And vowed he'd steal no more.

Traditional

The Queen was sad when the Knave stole the tarts. Trace the heart. Draw a sad face on it. Then color the heart blue.

The Queen was happy when the Knave brought the tarts back. Trace the heart. Draw a happy face on it. Then color the heart red.

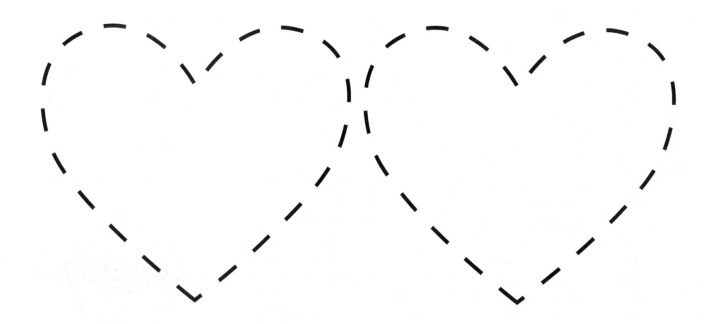

Abraham Lincoln and George Washington

═══════════════════════════ **DAY 1** ═══════════════════════════

Sharing Time: Talk about Abraham Lincoln, the 16th president, and why we celebrate his birthday. Point to Lincoln's birthday, February 12th, on a calendar. Read aloud a short biographical sketch about Lincoln (page 161).

Movement Activity: Have students practice "Presidents" (page 160) all week.

Lesson: Lincoln's Story

   Materials: pencils, copies of page 162

   Directions: Read the direction lines. Have students respond by circling the pictures.

═══════════════════════════ **DAY 2** ═══════════════════════════

Sharing Time: Talk about George Washington, the first president, and why we celebrate his birthday. Point to February 22nd, Washington's birthday, on a calendar. Read aloud a short biographical sketch about Washington (page 161).

Lesson: George Washington's Cherry Tree

   Materials: green, brown, and red tempera paint; paintbrushes; aluminum pie pans; copies of page 163

   Directions: Have the children trace the 8s and write some by themselves. Tell them to paint the cherry tree. Allow the paint to dry. To put cherries on the tree, have the children dip a fingertip in red tempera paint and make eight prints amongst the leaves on the tree.

═══════════════════════════ **DAY 3** ═══════════════════════════

Lesson: Matching Skills

   Materials: markers, copies of page 164

   Directions: Have the children look at each row of the pictures and circle the two that are the same and put an X on the one that is different.

═══════════════════════════ **DAY 4** ═══════════════════════════

Sharing Time: Talk about the holiday known as Presidents' Day.

Lesson: Presidents' Day

   Materials: colored pencils, scissors, glue, copies of pages 165 and 166

   Directions: Have students color the pictures and glue the objects from page 166 under the correct president on page 165.

═══════════════════════════ **DAY 5** ═══════════════════════════

Cooking Experience: Washington's Cherry Pie

   Materials: can of biscuits, can of cherry pie filling, whipped cream, cookie sheet, spray oil, spatula, plastic spoons, paper plates

   Directions: Have the children shape a biscuit to look like a pie crust. Place the biscuits on the sprayed cookie sheet. Have each child spoon cherry pie filling into the biscuit. Bake the biscuits in an oven set at 350 degrees Fahrenheit (175 degrees Celsius) for about 12 minutes or until the bottoms of the biscuits are golden brown. Let them cool for a few minutes. Top with whipped cream before serving them.

Presidents

Movement Activity

Who lived in a log cabin?

(Hold the tips of fingers from both hands together to form a roof.)

Who loved to read books?

(Open and shut hands like a book.)

Whose face is on a penny?

(Hold up a penny.)

Abraham Lincoln, the 16th President!

Who chopped down a cherry tree?

(Make a chopping motion with hands.)

Who loved to ride horses?

(Pretend to ride a horse.)

Whose face is on a quarter?

(Hold up a quarter.)

George Washington, the first President!

Deanna Reynolds

Name: _____ Date: _____

Abraham Lincoln

Abraham Lincoln was born in a log cabin in Kentucky. As a young boy, whenever he wasn't working on the family farm, he went to school. There, he learned to read. His favorite book was the Bible. He loved to learn new things and preferred going to school to doing chores on the farm. As a young man, Abraham worked as a storekeeper, a surveyor (a person who measures the land and draws maps), and a postmaster. People were impressed by his honesty and started calling him "Honest Abe." School was very important to him. While he worked as an Illinois legislator, he studied hard and became a lawyer. Abraham married a woman named Mary. They had four children. The American people knew that Abraham was an honest person and a hard worker. They elected Abraham Lincoln to be the 16th president.

Which coin and dollar bill has Abraham Lincoln's face on it? *(penny, five dollar bill)*

George Washington

When George Washington was a little boy, he liked to play outside and go to school to learn. As George grew up in Virginia, he rode his horse in races. He won many of those races. When George was a young man, he became a land surveyor. That meant he measured the land and drew maps. He married a woman named Martha. He worked as a farmer. Many Americans wanted to be free from English rulers. When war started between America and England, George became a general in the American Army. He was in charge of many soldiers. During the war, he was a very brave and wise leader. He even helped his troops survive a very cold and snowy winter. After America won the war, almost everyone knew about George and his wartime achievements. The people wanted him to lead America, now that it was its own country. George Washington became the first president. People started calling him the "Father of Our Country."

Which coin and dollar bill has George Washington's face on it? *(quarter, one dollar bill)*

Name: _____ Date: _____

Lincoln's Story

1. Circle the picture that shows who this story was about.

2. Circle the type of house in which Abraham was born.

3. Circle the picture of a job that Abraham did.

Name: _____ Date: _____

George Washington's Cherry Tree

There is a story that George Washington chopped down a cherry tree. Paint the tree. Let the paint dry. Then put 8 red cherries on the tree.

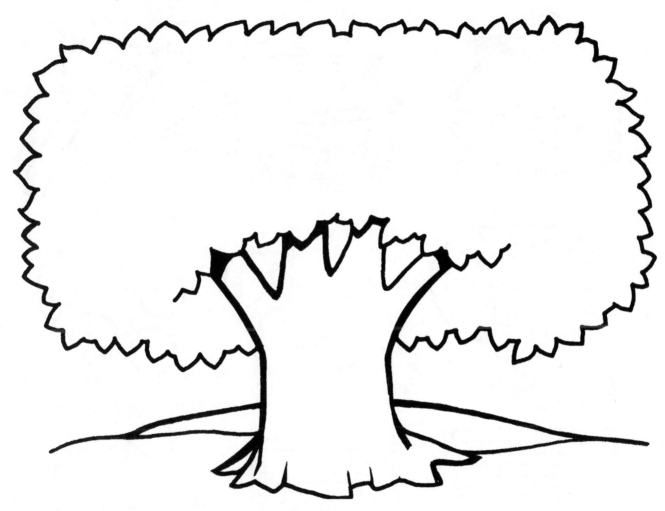

Trace the 8s. Then write some by yourself.

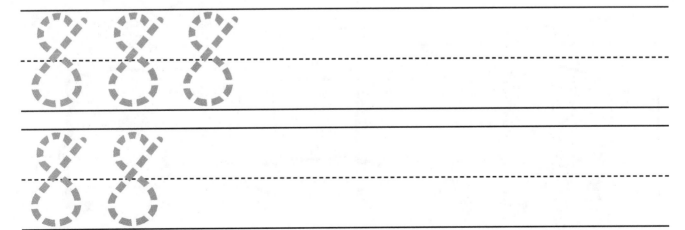

Name: _____ Date: _____

Matching Skills

Circle the pictures that match in each row. Write an X on the picture that does not match.

Name: _____ Date: _____

Presidents' Day

Cut out the pictures from page 166. Four of the pictures go with George Washington. Glue these under George's picture on this page. Four of the pictures go with Abraham Lincoln. Glue these under Abraham's picture on this page.

George Washington

Abraham Lincoln

Name: _____ Date: _____

Presidents' Day *(cont.)*

Cut out the pictures shown below. Glue them onto page 165.

March

Sunday	Monday	Tuesday	Wednesday	Thursday	Friday	Saturday

Winds and Phone Numbers

DAY 1

Sharing Time: Talk about the wind and how things move when the wind blows. If the wind is blowing, take the children outside with some objects, such as papers, rocks, and balloons. If the wind is not blowing, use a small fan. Let the children see which objects the wind can blow.

Lesson: Wind Power

    Materials: crayons, balloons, papers, rocks, small fan, copies of page 169

    Directions: Have the children color the picture of the objects that can be moved by wind. Have them put an X on the pictures that cannot be moved by wind.

DAY 2

Sharing Time: Discuss the meaning of "March roars in like a lion and goes out like a lamb."

Lesson: Lion and Lamb

    Materials: crayons, yellow yarn, white cotton balls, scissors, glue, copies of page 170

    Directions: Tell students to glue pieces of yellow yarn onto the lion's mane. Have them glue white cotton balls to make the lamb's wool. Then invite them to color the rest of the picture.

DAY 3

Sharing Time: Invite students to tell about personal experiences with the wind.

Lesson: March Wind

    Materials: markers, copies of page 171

    Directions: Ask students to draw a line to show the path from the wind to the balloon. Point out that there is only one correct path.

DAY 4

Sharing Time: Discuss the importance of students knowing their phone numbers. Have them practice every day to memorize their phone numbers.

Lesson: My Phone Number

    Materials: watercolors, scissors, copies of page 172

    Directions: Write a child's name and phone number on the phones. Have the children paint and cut out the phones. Allow time for the children to practice saying their phone numbers.

DAY 5

Cooking Experience: Lion Salad and Lamb Cupcakes

    Materials: paper plates, plastic knives, can of halved peaches, coconut, raisins, tube of red gel icing, white frosted snack cakes, vanilla wafers, white frosting

    Directions: On each child's plate, place a peach half with the curved side up. Sprinkle coconut around it for the lion's mane. Have them push raisins into the peach for the nose and eyes and draw a mouth using red gel icing. Next give each child a white snack cake. Have them make the sheep's ears by gently pushing two vanilla wafers into the top of the cake. Have them frost the wafers with white icing. Then have them use raisins for eyes and nose and red gel icing for the mouth.

Name: _____ Date: _____

Wind Power

Color the picture of the objects that can be moved by wind. Put an X on the pictures that cannot be moved by wind.

Name: _____ Date: _____

Lion and Lamb

"March roars in like a lion and goes out like a lamb."

Glue pieces of yellow yarn to make the lion's mane. Glue white cotton balls to make the lamb's wool. Color the rest of the picture.

Name: _____ Date: _____

March Wind

The wind wants to blow away the balloon. Help the wind find the right path to the balloon. Draw a line from the wind to the balloon. Then color the picture.

Name: _____ Date: _____

My Phone Number

Paint the phone with watercolors. Cut it out, and hang it up. Practice saying your phone number every day.

Name

Phone Number

St. Patrick's Day

The lesson plan suggested below is organized for a week with St. Patrick's Day falling on Wednesday. Arrange the week's activities around the day on which March 17th falls. If this holiday occurs on a weekend, plan to do the DAY 3 activities on the preceding Friday.

═══ DAY 1 ═══

Sharing Time: Read aloud stories about Leprechauns and shamrocks. Locate Ireland on a map and talk about it. Ask students to brainstorm a list of things that are green.

Arts and Crafts: Shamrock

> **Materials:** green crayon or marker, green watercolors, paintbrushes, copies of page 174

> **Directions:** Have the children trace the shamrock with a green crayon or marker. Then have them paint it with green watercolor.

═══ DAY 2 ═══

Arts and Crafts: Potato Painting

> **Materials:** potatoes, crayons, green tempera paint, aluminum pie pans, copies of page 175

> **Directions:** Cut the potatoes in half and carve shapes, such as a diamond or shamrock, into the flat surface of each. Have students use the potatoes to stamp paint onto the shamrock.

═══ DAY 3 ═══

Sharing Time: St. Patrick's Day

Before students arrive, place tiny shoe prints around the classroom leading to a pot filled with treats. When the children arrive, tell them to follow the leprechaun's shoe prints to the pot.

Game: Hot Gold Coin

Make a large gold coin using poster board, glue, and glitter. Have the children stand in a circle and pass the coin until the music stops. The child holding the coin is out of the game. Continue playing until only one child is left.

═══ DAY 4 ═══

Lesson: The Leprechaun's Gold

> **Materials:** crayons, scissors, glue and gold glitter, copies of page 176

> **Directions:** Have the children trace the number 9 on the leprechaun's pot of gold. Allow them to color the leprechaun. Ask the children to smear glue on the coins in the pot and sprinkle gold glitter onto the glue.

═══ DAY 5 ═══

Cooking Experience: Green Eggs and Ham

> **Materials:** skillet, butter, spatula, paper plates, plastic forks, plastic spoons, thinly sliced ham, eggs, green food coloring, shredded cheese (optional)

> **Directions:** Heat the skillet and melt the butter. Help each child break an egg into the skillet. After all the eggs are in the skillet, let each child take a turn stirring the eggs. Add the ham and food coloring. Cook the eggs until they are done. Add cheese, if desired. Then serve.

Name: _____ Date: _____

Shamrock

Trace the shamrock. Paint the shamrock green.

Name: _____ Date: _____

Potato Painting

Make stamps from pieces of potato. Dip the stamps in green paint. Then stamp the paint onto the shamrock.

Name: _____ Date: _____

The Leprechaun's Gold

Trace the number 9 on the leprechaun's pot of gold. Color the leprechaun. Count the coins in the pot. Smear glue on the coins. Then sprinkle gold glitter onto the glue. Allow the glue to dry. Shake off any extra glitter.

176

Kites and Clouds

DAY 1

Sharing Time: Talk about clouds and the winds that occur in the spring. Explain that windy days are good kite-flying weather.

Movement Activity: Have students practice "Five Little Kites" (page 178) all week.

Lesson: Matching Kites

    Materials: colored pencils, crayons, or markers; copies of page 179

    Directions: Have the children draw lines to match the uppercase letters with the lowercase letters on the kites. Then encourage students to color the pairs of kites.

DAY 2

Sharing Time: Caution students against looking at the sun. Then go outside and have the them look at the clouds. Talk about the different shapes they see.

Arts and Crafts: Cloud Necklaces

    Materials: crayons, scissors, colored yarn, hole punch, white cotton balls, glue, copies of page 180

    Directions: Have students make cloud necklaces using the directions on page 180.

DAY 3

Sharing Time: Point out that some things go up in the sky and others stay on the ground.

Lesson: Up and Down

    Materials: colored pencils, crayons, scissors, glue, copies of pages 181 and 182

    Directions: Have the children color the pictures on pages 181 and 182. Have them glue the things that go up in the sky near the kite and the things that go down on the ground near the worms.

DAY 4

Arts and Crafts: Kite Windsock

    Materials: construction paper, various colors; yarn; hole punch; scissors; crayons; markers; glue; crepe paper steamers, various colors

    Directions: Draw kite shapes onto pieces of colored construction paper. Have the children decorate the kites and cut them out. Then have them glue crepe paper streamers onto the bottom of the kite. Help them punch a hole in the top of each kite. String a piece of yarn through the hole to hang up the windsock. Let it blow in the breeze.

DAY 5

Cooking Experience: Clouds in the Sky Pudding

    Materials: package of vanilla pudding; milk; mixing bowls; measuring cup; wire whisk; blue food coloring; whipped cream; plastic bowls, one per child; plastic spoons

    Directions: Make pudding by following the directions on the package. Have the children add blue food coloring to make it look like the sky. Pour the pudding into the bowls. Add spoonfuls of whipped cream to the top to form the clouds in the sky.

Five Little Kites

Movement Activity

Five little kites blowing in the wind.

(Spread fingers apart. Sway hand in the air like a kite.)

One flew away, and now there are four.

Four little kites blowing in the wind.

(Spread four fingers apart. Hide thumb. Sway hand in the air like a kite.)

One fell to the ground, and now there are three.

Three little kites blowing in the wind.

(Hold three fingers apart. Hide thumb and index finger. Sway hand in the air like a kite.)

One went tumbling into a tree, and now there are two.

Two little kites blowing in the wind.

(Spread two fingers apart. Sway hand in the air like a kite.)

One flew to the sun, and now there is one.

One little kite blowing in the wind.

(Hold up one finger. Sway hand in the air like a kite.)

One little kite followed you home, and now there are none.

(Show a zero with fingers.)

Deanna Reynolds

Name: _____ Date: _____

Matching Kites

Draw lines to match the uppercase letters with the lowercase letters. Then color each pair of kites.

Name: _____ Date: _____

Cloud Necklaces

Have students choose a pattern for a cloud necklace. Have them cut out the pattern. Tell them to glue cotton onto the pattern so that it looks like a cloud. Punch a hole where indicated. String a piece of yarn through the hole and tie the ends together. Encourage students to wear their necklaces.

Name: _____ Date: _____

Up and Down

The kite is flying up in the sky, and the little worms are down in the grass on the ground. Cut out the pictures on page 182. Glue the things that go up in the sky near the kite. Glue the things that go down on the ground near the worms.

Name: _____ Date: _____

Up and Down (cont.)

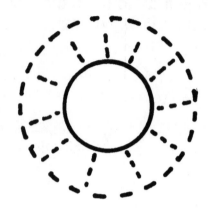

Money

=== **DAY 1** ===

Sharing Time: Talk about money and how it is used to buy things. Show a penny, nickel, dime, and quarter. Teach the names and values of these coins.

Lesson: Money

    Materials: colored pencils or markers, copies of page 184

    Directions: Help students tell the name and value of each coin. Have them determine how many cents are in each box. Tell them to draw a circle around the correct amount.

=== **DAY 2** ===

Sharing Time: Tell how money is used to buy things like food, clothes, toys, etc. Talk about the different coins and have them learn the value of each coin.

Lesson: Toy Store

    Materials: colored pencils, markers or crayons, copies of page 185

    Directions: Tell the children that in this activity they are pretending to buy toys. Have them draw a circle around the coins that they would need to buy each item.

=== **DAY 3** ===

Lesson: Yard Sale

    Materials: colored pencils, markers or crayons, copies of page 186

    Directions: Have the children pretend they are buying the toys at a yard sale. They need to circle the coins that add up to the price of the toys.

=== **DAY 4** ===

Sharing Time: Review talking about coins, values of coins, and what you can buy with them.

Arts and Crafts: Coin Bracelet

    Materials: clear contact paper, pennies, hole punch, yarn

    Directions: Cut clear contact paper into strips wide enough to fully cover a penny and long enough to fit around a child's wrist. Help the children peel off the backing from the contact paper. Have them lay the contact paper on the table, sticky side up. Next, let them place 1–3 pennies in a line on the sticky side of the contact paper. Help the children fold the contact paper until the pennies are fully encased in it. Punch a hole into the ends of the contact paper. Then use a piece of yarn to tie the bracelet onto the child's wrist.

=== **DAY 5** ===

Cooking Experience: Golden Coins

    Materials: skillet, 1/2 cup (125 mL) butter (Use more if needed.), tongs, plate, paper plates, plastic knives, powdered sugar, 1/2 banana per child

    Directions: Melt the butter in the skillet. Have the children use plastic knives to cut their banana halves into slices. Put the slices in the hot skillet, turning them until both sides are golden. After cooking the banana coins, place them onto a plate of powdered sugar. Coat both sides, cool, and serve.

Name: _____ Date: _____

Money

Learn to recognize the penny, nickel, dime, and quarter and tell how much they are worth.

penny	nickel	dime	quarter

1 cent	5 cents	10 cents	25 cents
1¢	5¢	10¢	25¢

How many cents are in each box? Draw a circle around the correct amount.

A.	B.
7¢ 3¢ 9¢	7¢ 8¢ 9¢

C.	D.
6¢ 10¢ 1¢	3¢ 25¢ 1¢

E.	F.
10¢ 4¢ 3¢	25¢ 5¢ 10¢

G.	H.
5¢ 10¢ 6¢	4¢ 5¢ 25¢

Name: _____ Date: _____

Toy Store

Look at the different coins. Each coin is worth a different amount of money.

penny	**nickel**	**dime**	**quarter**

1 cent	5 cents	10 cents	25 cents
1¢	5¢	10¢	25¢

Draw a circle around the coins that you would need to buy each item.

A.

B.

C.

D.

Name: _____ Date: _____

Yard Sale

Draw a circle around the coins that you would need to buy each item.

A.

B.

C.

D.

Easter

Easter is celebrated in either March or April. Use the lesson plans the week of Easter.

═══ DAY 1 ═══

Sharing Time: Talk about Easter and many of the things associated with Easter, such as eggs, rabbits, chicks, and candies.

Movement Activity: Have students practice "Five Easter Bunnies" or "Easter Bunny" (page 189) all week.

Lesson: Easter Eggs

Materials: colored pencils or markers, copies of page 190

Directions: Have the children find and circle the ten Easter eggs in the picture. Then invite them to color the picture.

(Answers: three eggs in the tree, two eggs on two of the rabbits' tails, one egg in the basket, one egg in the bush by the tree, three eggs in the centers of the flowers)

═══ DAY 2 ═══

Sharing Time: Continue talking about Easter and the traditions associated with this holiday.

Lesson: Easter Candy

Materials: colored pencils, markers, or crayons; copies of page 191

Directions: Have the children count and circle the number in each box that shows how many Easter candies there are.

═══ DAY 3 ═══

Sharing Time: Using the Easter theme, talk about things that are full and empty. Have Easter baskets to show what empty means and then fill them with plastic eggs to show what full means.

Lesson: Easter Basket and Eggs

Materials: crayons or markers, glue, scissors, watercolors, paintbrushes, copies of pages 192 and 193, cellophane grass (optional)

Directions: Allow the children to decorate the basket using crayons or markers. Tell them to paint the eggs using the watercolors. After the paint has dried, have the children cut out the eggs and glue them in the Easter basket.

Option: You may wish to have the children glue cellophane grass in the basket. Then they can glue the eggs onto the cellophane grass.

Easter *(cont.)*

═══════════════════ **DAY 4** ═══════════════════

Sharing Time: Talk abut Easter baskets and how they are used to collect Easter eggs.

Arts and Crafts: Easter Basket

> **Materials:** plastic berry baskets; pipe cleaners; cellophane grass; ribbon or crepe paper streamers, various colors

> **Directions:** Collect enough berry baskets so that you have one for each child. You can save the baskets throughout the year or send a note home asking parents to send some with their children. Have each child weave ribbon or crepe paper streamers in and out through the holes at the top of each basket. Have the children twist two pipe cleaners together to make the handles of the baskets. Then tell them to fill the baskets with cellophane grass and leave it for the Easter bunny to fill with treats. You may wish to have the children use these baskets on DAY 5 for the Easter egg hunt.

═══════════════════ **DAY 5** ═══════════════════

Cooking Experience: Baby Chicks

> **Materials:** one hard-boiled egg per child, paper plates, plastic knives, plastic spoons, bowl, large spoon, mayonnaise, vinegar, mustard, raisins, carrot slivers, coconut, food coloring

> **Directions:** Dye the coconut according to the following directions: Put ½–1 cup (125–250 mL) of coconut into a resealable plastic bag. Add a few drops of the desired food coloring (red, green, yellow, blue). Seal the plastic bag and shake it until the coconut is coated with the food coloring. Open the plastic bag and let the coconut air dry for 30 minutes. After it has dried, it is ready to use. Have the children put some colored coconut on their paper plates. Let each child peel a hard-boiled egg, cut it in half, and take out the yolk. Show them how to place each egg half, flat side up, in the green coconut. Put all the yolks in a bowl. Ask a volunteer to stir in enough mayonnaise and vinegar to make a thick mixture. Then add a small amount of mustard to make the mixture yellow. Have each child take a spoonful and put it into each egg half. Then have the children use the raisins for the eyes and the carrot slivers for the beak.

Easter Egg Hunt:

Before the children arrive, fill plastic eggs with jellybeans. Hide the eggs outside if the weather permits. Otherwise hide them inside. Before beginning the hunt, tell the children how many eggs they are allowed to find. Stress that they should not gather more than this amount so that everyone gets some of the eggs.

Easter Bunny

Easter bunny hop around.
(Hop like a bunny.)
Easter bunny shake your ears.
*(Hold hands behind head like bunny ears, and move hands
back and forth.)*
Easter bunny wiggle your nose.
(Wiggle your nose.)
Easter bunny crunch a carrot.
(Crunch on a carrot.)
Easter bunny rest your head.
(Place palms of hands together. Rest head on hands.)

Deanna Reynolds

Five Easter Bunnies

Five Easter bunnies getting ready for Easter
(Hold up five fingers.)
First one said, "The Easter eggs are ready!"
(Hold up one finger and point to watch.)
Second one said, "The Easter candy is here!"
(Hold up two fingers and point to pretend candy.)
Third one said, "Let's fill the Easter baskets!"
(Hold up three fingers. Then pretend to fill Easter baskets.)
Fourth one said, "It's time to get hopping!"
(Hold up four fingers. Then hop like a bunny.)
Fifth one said, "It's time to deliver!"
*(Hold up five fingers. Then hop while holding imaginary basket and
pretend to deliver eggs.)*

Deanna Reynolds

Name: _____ Date: _____

Easter Eggs

The Easter bunnies are looking for Easter eggs. Help the bunnies by finding and circling ten Easter eggs. Then color the picture.

Name: _____ Date: _____

Easter Candy

The Easter Bunny is counting candies for some children's Easter baskets. Circle the number in each box that shows how many candies the Easter Bunny has counted.

2   4   6

1   3   5

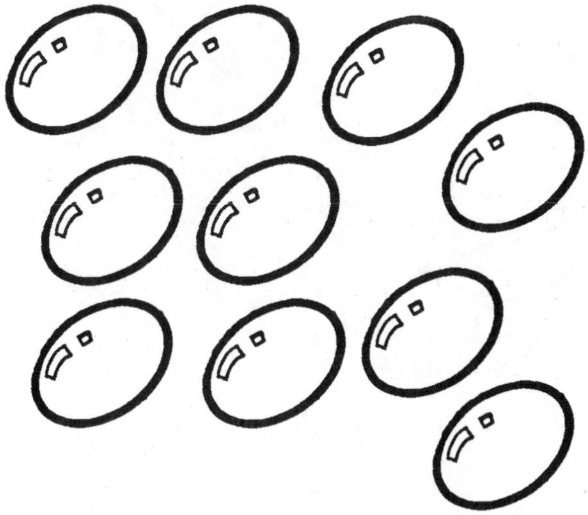

8   9   10

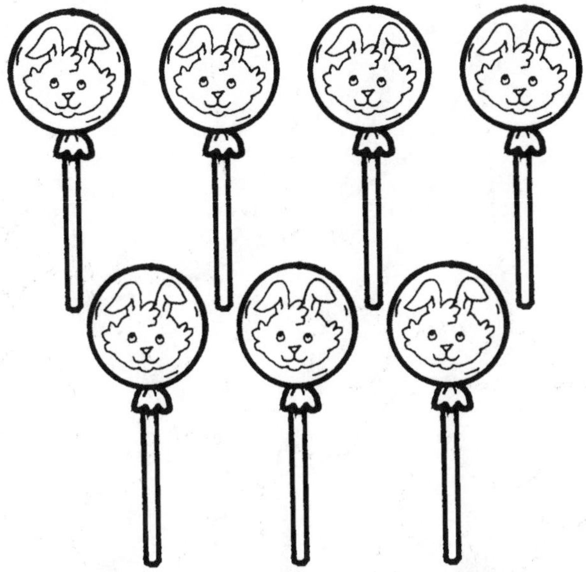

7   8   9

Name: _____ Date: _____

Easter Basket and Eggs

Color the Easter basket. Fill it with the Easter eggs from page 193.

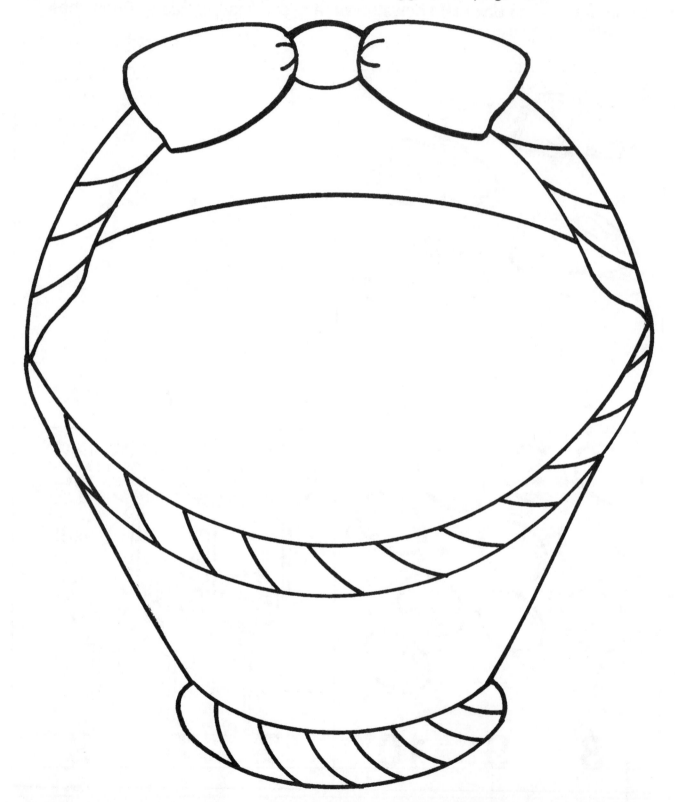

Name: _____ Date: _____

Easter Basket and Eggs *(cont.)*

Paint the Easter eggs with watercolors. Cut the eggs out and glue them into the basket on page 192.

April

	Sunday	Monday	Tuesday	Wednesday	Thursday	Friday	Saturday

Rain Showers and Rainbows

═══════════════════════ **DAY 1** ═══════════════════════

Sharing Time: Talk about rain, raindrops, and rainbows. Ask students to name some changes that they have noticed during the spring. Examples: rainstorm, rainbows, flowers blooming.

Movement Activity: Have students practice "Raindrops" (page 196) all week.

Lesson: April Showers

　　Materials: colored pencils or fine-point markers, copies of page 197

　　Directions: Have the children use the numbers to connect the dots in the right order. Ask them to tell what the bunny is holding.

═══════════════════════ **DAY 2** ═══════════════════════

Sharing Time: Read aloud some stories about springtime, rain showers, and/or rainbows.

Lesson: April Numbers

　　Materials: colored pencils, copies of page 198

　　Directions: Have the children count the items in each box. Tell them to circle the number that shows how many items there are.

═══════════════════════ **DAY 3** ═══════════════════════

Arts and Crafts: Rainy Days

　　Materials: blue construction paper; magazine pictures of animals, flowers, children, etc.; silver glitter; glue; scissors; crayons or markers

　　Directions: Provide blue construction paper and a variety of magazines for students. Tell them to make a spring scene by cutting out and gluing pictures or drawing pictures. Have them smear glue and sprinkle glitter to make raindrops.

═══════════════════════ **DAY 4** ═══════════════════════

Sharing Time: Teach children the colors of the rainbow — ROY G. BIV (red, orange, yellow, green, blue, indigo, violet).

Lesson: Make a Rainbow

　　Materials: small colored paper plates; crepe-paper streamers (in the colors listed above); glue; scissors; crayons or markers

　　Directions: Cut the paper plates in half. Give each child half of a plate. Have the children draw a smiling face on the plate. Then have them glue on the different colored crepe paper streamers to be the rainbow's colors.

═══════════════════════ **DAY 5** ═══════════════════════

Cooking Experience: Rainbow Pudding

　　Materials: bowl, wire whisk, large spoon, measuring cup, package of vanilla pudding, small plastic bowls, plastic spoon, food coloring

　　Directions: Make the pudding using the directions on the package. Pour pudding into cups. Then add drops of food coloring and ask the children to gently stir in the food coloring.

Raindrops

Movement Activity

This is the sun

(Form circle with arms.)

High in the sky.

(Hold arms in circle high above head.)

Here comes a dark cloud

(Sweep arms.)

Sailing by.

(Sweep arms side by side.)

These are the raindrops

(Flutter fingers down.)

Pitter-pattering down.

(Flutter fingers down.)

They water the flowers

(Hold hands like flowers.)

That grow in the ground.

(Cup hands.)

Traditional

Name: _____ Date: _____

April Showers

Use the numbers to connect the dots in the right order. See what the bunny is holding to stay dry in the rain.

Name: _____ Date: _____

April Numbers

Count the items in each box. Circle the number that shows how many items
there are.

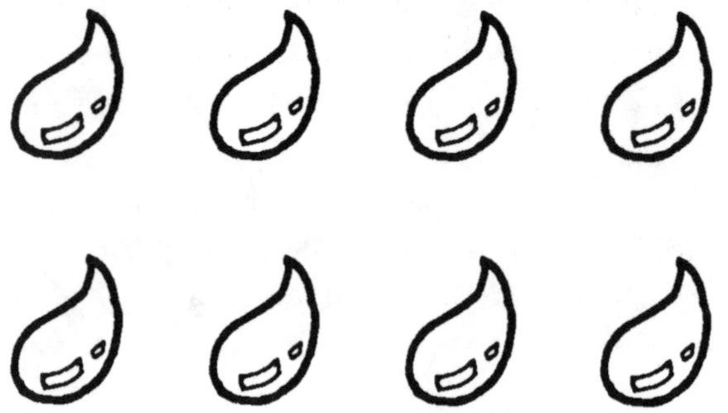

7 **8** **9**	**5** **6** **7**
6 **7** **8**	**8** **9** **10**
4 **5** **6**	**8** **9** **10**

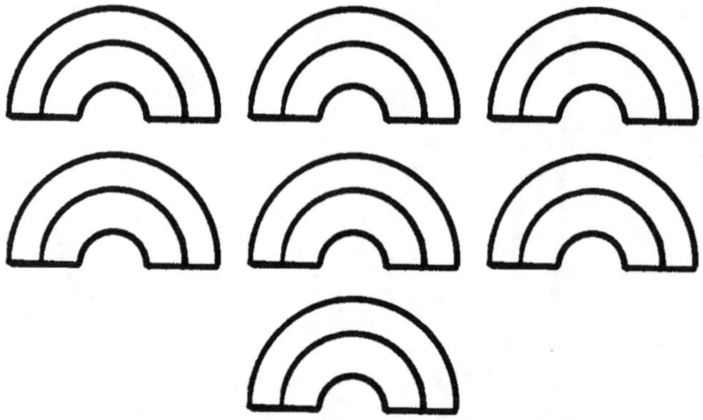

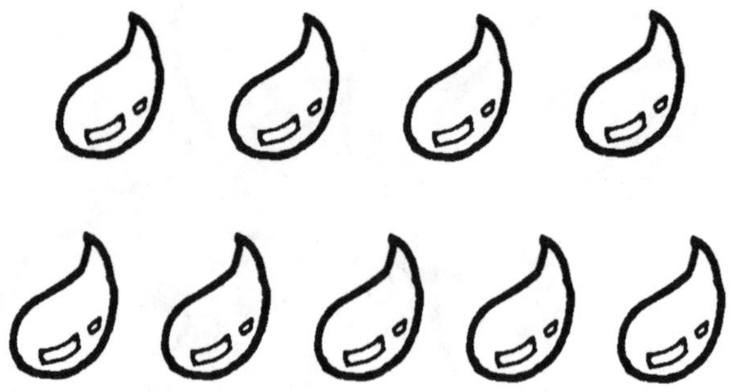

Spring Flowers and Honeybees

═══════════════════════ **DAY 1** ═══════════════════════

Sharing Time: Talk about spring. If possible, take a walk to look for signs of spring.

Arts and Crafts: Springtime Suncatcher

Materials: two identical clear contact paper shapes, such as circles, diamonds, triangles; glitter; real objects collected during the spring walk or springtime stickers; hole punch; yarn

Directions: For each child, cut two matching shapes from the contact paper. Have the children peel the backing off the contact paper and lay both pieces with the sticky side up. Tell them to put stickers or real objects (flowers, buds, leaves) and glitter on one piece of contact paper. Have them place the other piece of contact paper on top with the sticky sides together. Help the children seal the edges. Next have the children punch a hole close to the edge. String a piece of yarn through the hole and hang the suncatcher in a window.

═══════════════════════ **DAY 2** ═══════════════════════

Sharing Time: Discuss honeybees, how they collect pollen, and how they make honey.

Movement Activity: Have students practice "Here Is the Beehive" (page 200) all week.

Lesson: Honeybees

Materials: colored pencils, copies of page 201

Directions: Have students trace the numbers to show how many bees are in each group.

═══════════════════════ **DAY 3** ═══════════════════════

Lesson: Springtime

Materials: colored pencils or crayons, copies of page 202

Directions: Have the children trace the lines from the bees to the flowers.

═══════════════════════ **DAY 4** ═══════════════════════

Arts and Crafts: Tissue Flowers

Materials: tissue paper circles with 6" (15 cm) diameter, various colors; green pipe cleaners

Directions: Give each child three tissue paper circles. Put the tissue paper together and pull down the centers about 1" (2.5 cm). Help the children wrap a green pipe cleaner around the part that is pulled down. Tell them that this part is the flower's stem.

═══════════════════════ **DAY 5** ═══════════════════════

Cooking Experience: Edible Honeybees

Materials: ½ cup (125 mL) of peanut butter, 2 tablespoons (30 mL) honey, 2 tablespoons (30 mL) sesame seeds, ⅓ cup (90 mL) powdered milk, sliced almonds, chocolate syrup, measuring cups, measuring spoons, toothpicks, large bowl, wooden spoon, small paper cups, wax paper

Directions: In the bowl, mix together the peanut butter, honey, sesame seeds, and powdered milk. Give each child a square of wax paper with a spoonful of the mixture. Have the children shape the mixture into a bee shape. Pour chocolate syrup into small cups. Let them use a toothpick and the syrup to draw the bee's face and to make stripes on the bee's body. Have them use two almond slices for each bee's wings.

Here Is the Beehive

Movement Activity

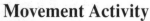

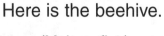
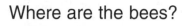
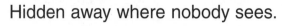

Here is the beehive.

(Make a fist.)

Where are the bees?

(Shrug shoulders.)

Hidden away where nobody sees.

(Show fist.)

Here they come buzzing

(Open fist slowly.)

Out of the hive — 1, 2, 3, 4, 5.

(Hold up fingers to match the numbers counted.)

Traditional

Name: _____ Date: _____

Honeybees

Count each group of bees going to the hive. Trace the number that shows how many bees are in each group.

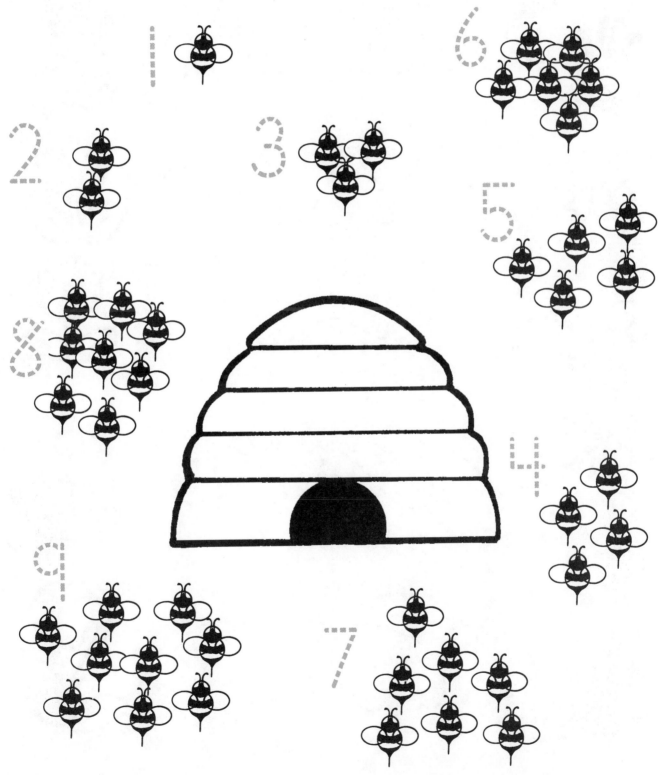

Name: _____ Date: _____

Springtime

Trace the lines from the bees to the flowers. Then color the pictures.

Ladybugs

═══════════════════════════ **DAY 1** ═══════════════════════════

Sharing Time: Talk about ladybugs, the spots they have, and how small they are.

Movement Activity: Have students practice "Little Ladybug" (page 204) all week.

Lesson: Where Are the Ladybugs?

   Materials: colored pencils or crayons, copies of page 205

   Directions: Have the children find and circle 10 ladybugs.

═══════════════════════════ **DAY 2** ═══════════════════════════

Sharing Time: Review the letters of the alphabet — uppercase and lowercase.

Lesson: Ladybug Letters

   Materials: crayons or markers, copies of page 206

   Directions: Have the children draw lines to match the uppercase and lowercase letters. Then tell them to color the ladybugs.

═══════════════════════════ **DAY 3** ═══════════════════════════

Sharing Time: Review the numbers 1–10

Lesson: Ladybug Numbers

   Materials: colored pencils or fine-point markers, copies of page 207

   Directions: Ask students to count the number of spots on each ladybug. Tell them to trace the numbers and write some by themselves. Then have them color the ladybugs.

═══════════════════════════ **DAY 4** ═══════════════════════════

Lesson: Ladybug's Favorite Number

   Materials: watercolors, crayons, glue, scissors, brads, copies of page 208

   Directions: Have the children write their favorite number (1–10) onto the ladybug's body. Then have them color that number of spots on the wings. Tell them to paint the ladybug using watercolors. Then have them cut out the parts. Show the children how to glue the antennae on the ladybug's head and use a brad pushed through the X's to connect the wings to the body.

═══════════════════════════ **DAY 5** ═══════════════════════════

Cooking Experience: Ladybug Cookies

   Materials: pre-made sugar cookie dough, cookie sheet, cooking spray, paper plates, plastic knives, white frosting, red food dye, chocolate frosting, chocolate chips, thin black licorice cut into 3" (7.5 cm) pieces

   Directions: Bake the cookies and cool them. Dye the white frosting red and let the children frost ¾ of the cookie. Frost the other ⅓ cookie with the chocolate frosting. To make the ladybug's spots, use chocolate chips. The licorice is used for the stripe down the ladybug's back and for the antennae. For the eyes, use two chocolate chips.

Little Ladybug
Movement Activity

A little ladybug is flying to me.
(Use pinkie finger to be ladybug. Fly toward body.)

A little ladybug is landing on my nose.
(Land pinkie finger on nose.)

A little ladybug is landing on my toes.
(Land pinkie finger on toes.)

A little ladybug is landing on my knee.
(Land pinkie finger on knee.)

A little ladybug is landing on my elbow.
(Land pinkie finger on elbow.)

A little ladybug is flying away.
(Move pinkie finger away from body.)

Amberly Reynolds

   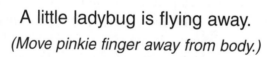

Where Are the Ladybugs?

Name: _____ Date: _____

Find 10 ladybugs and circle them. Then color the picture.

Ladybug Letters

Name: _____ Date: _____

Draw lines to match the uppercase and lowercase letters. Then color the ladybugs.

Ladybug Numbers

Name: _____ Date: _____

Count the number of spots on each ladybug. Trace the numbers. Write some by yourself. Then color the ladybugs.

8 _____   5 _____   3 _____

1 _____   6 _____   4 _____

9 _____   2 _____   7 _____

10 _____

Name: _____ Date: _____

Ladybug's Favorite Number

Write your favorite number (1–10) on the body of the ladybug. Color that number of spots. Paint the ladybug using watercolors. Then cut out the parts and put the ladybug together. Glue the antennae on the ladybug's head. Push a brad through the X's to connect the wings to the body.

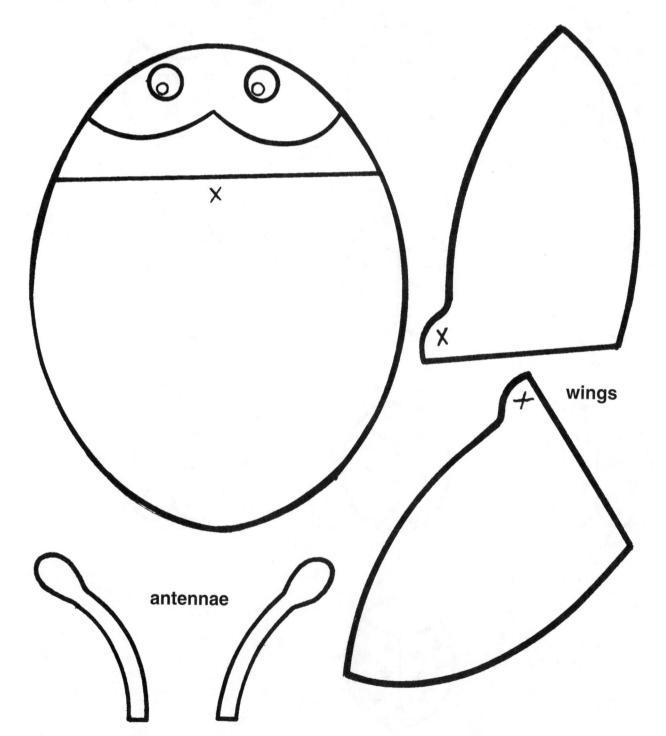

wings

antennae

Caterpillars and Butterflies

━━━━━━━━━━━━━━ **DAY 1** ━━━━━━━━━━━━━━

Sharing Time: Talk to the children about the life cycle of a caterpillar/butterfly.

Movement Activity: Have students practice "Caterpillar's Surprise" (page 210) all week.

Lesson: Butterfly Life Cycle

    Materials: crayons, watercolors, paintbrushes, scissors, brads, copies of pages 211 and 212

    Directions: Have the children color or use watercolors to paint both pages. Have them cut out both wheels and use a brad to put them together.

━━━━━━━━━━━━━━ **DAY 2** ━━━━━━━━━━━━━━

Sharing Time: Have the children tell the sequence of events in a butterfly's life cycle. Share books about caterpillars and butterflies with the class.

Arts and Crafts: Pom Pom Caterpillar

    Materials: green poster board, ½" (1.25 cm) green pom poms, small eyes, green pipe cleaner, glue, scissors, page 213

    Directions: Trace the leaf pattern onto green poster board, making one per child. Have the children cut out their leaves. Then have them use four or five green pom poms and glue them in a line on the leaf. Have the children glue two eyes onto the first pom pom. Then help them bend and glue a 1" (2.5 cm) green pipe cleaner for the antennae.

━━━━━━━━━━━━━━ **DAY 3** ━━━━━━━━━━━━━━

Sharing Time: Talk about different kinds of butterflies.

Arts and Crafts: Drip Drop Butterfly

    Materials: scissors; tempera paint, various colors; paintbrushes; copies of page 214

    Directions: Cut out the butterflies. On one side of the butterflies, have the children use paintbrushes to drip different colors of paint onto the butterfly. Tell them to fold the butterfly in half and gently rub it to mix the paint. Have them open it slowly.

━━━━━━━━━━━━━━ **DAY 4** ━━━━━━━━━━━━━━

Arts and Crafts: Butterfly Mobile

    Materials: poster board, various colors; yarn; hole punch; scissors; stapler; crayons or watercolors; paintbrushes; copies of page 215

    Directions: Directions for the mobile frame appear on page 129. Have the children either color or use watercolors to paint the mobile pieces. Then have them cut out the pieces and use yarn to connect them to the frame.

━━━━━━━━━━━━━━ **DAY 5** ━━━━━━━━━━━━━━

Cooking Experience: Caterpillar Salad

    Materials: for each child — one piece of apple, two pieces of peach, three pieces of plum, four pieces of strawberry or whole strawberries, five pieces of orange, disposable long skewer

    Directions: Have the children place the fruit on the skewer in order of the number of pieces (1–5) just like in the story *The Very Hungry Caterpillar* by Eric Carle.

Caterpillar's Surprise

Movement Activity

A very small caterpillar started to eat leaves.

(Pretend to eat leaves.)

Then the caterpillar spun a cocoon.

(Spin around two times.)

The caterpillar took a long nap.

(Pretend to be asleep.)

Slowly the caterpillar breaks out to find a surprise.

(Stretch out arms and look surprised.)

It's now a beautiful butterfly and flies away.

(Move arms like wings and pretend to fly.)

Ashley Reynolds

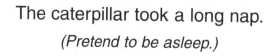
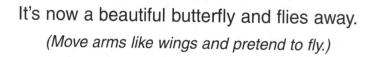

Name: _____ Date: _____

Butterfly Life Cycle

Color and cut out top wheel shown below. Cut out the wedge with the dotted lines. Color the pictures on page 212. Cut out the bottom wheel. Place the top wheel on the bottom wheel with the colored sides up. Push a brad through the centers of both wheels to hold the wheels together.

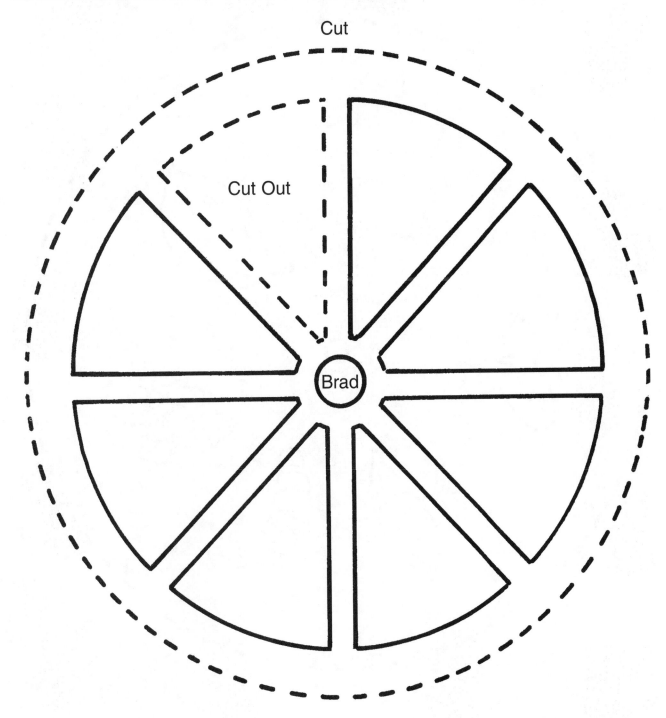

Name: _____ Date: _____

Butterfly Life Cycle (cont.)

Cut

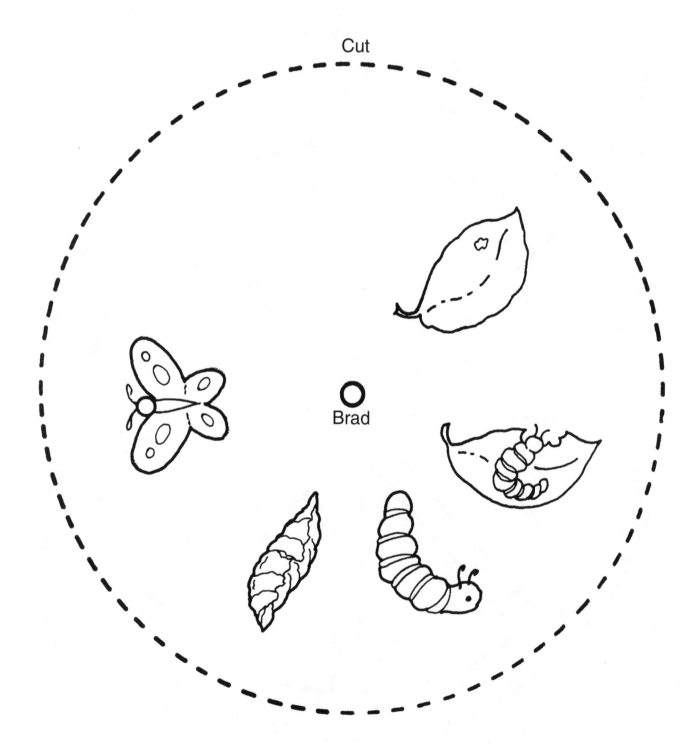

Brad

Name: _____   Date: _____

Leaf Pattern

Trace the leaf pattern onto green poster board, making one for each child. Let the children cut out their leaves and glue on a pom pom caterpillar.

Name: _____ Date: _____

Drip Drop Butterfly

Cut out the butterfly. Drip paint on one side. Fold the butterfly in half. Rub the wings together. Then open up the butterfly.

Name: _____   Date: _____

Butterfly Mobile

Color or use watercolors to paint the pieces of the mobile. Cut out all the pieces. Punch holes where shown. String a piece of yarn through each hole. Then attach it to the mobile frame.

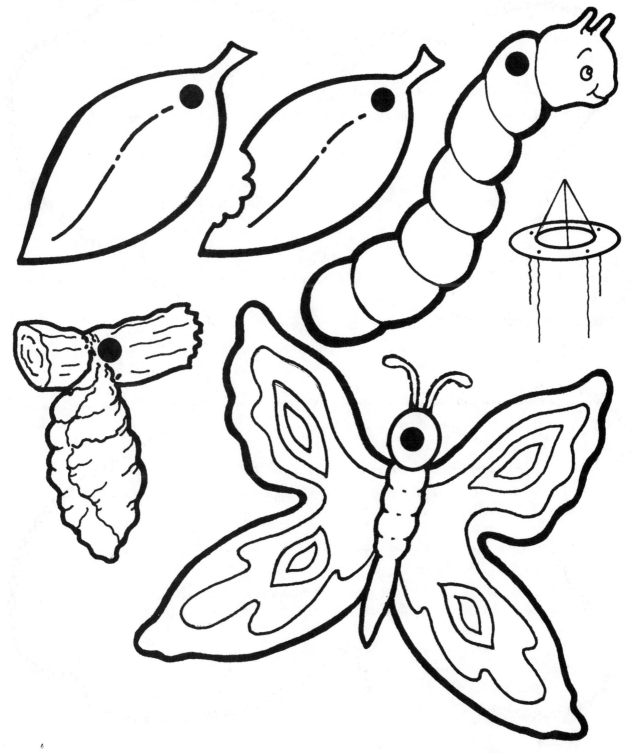

Birds

═══════════════════ **DAY 1** ═══════════════════

Sharing Time: Talk about the different kinds of birds, nests, and eggs there are. Talk about how some birds migrate.

Lesson: Birds Everywhere

 Materials: crayons, markers or colored pencils, copies of page 217

 Directions: Have the children trace the numbers on each of the birds. Next have them color each bird a different color.

═══════════════════ **DAY 2** ═══════════════════

Sharing Time: Try and have different kinds of books about birds to show how many different kinds and colors of birds there are.

Lesson: Match the Birds

 Materials: colored pencils, copies of page 218

 Directions: Have the children draw lines to match the birds that look alike. Then have them color the matching birds alike.

═══════════════════ **DAY 3** ═══════════════════

Sharing Time: Talk to the children about how birds make their nests and lay eggs.

Lesson: Nests and Eggs

 Materials: colored pencils or crayons, copies of page 219

 Directions: Have the children trace the number on each nest and draw the corresponding number of eggs in the nest. Allow them to color the picture.

═══════════════════ **DAY 4** ═══════════════════

Sharing Time: Have students tell about birds that they have seen.

Lesson: Letter Birds

 Materials: colored pencils or markers, copies of page 220

 Directions: Have students draw lines to match the uppercase letters on the birds with the lowercase letters on the worms.

═══════════════════ **DAY 5** ═══════════════════

Cooking Experience: Bird Nests and Eggs

 Materials: ½ cup (125 mL) of peanut butter, 2 tablespoons (30 mL) honey, 2 tablespoons (30 mL) sesame seeds, ⅓ cup (90 mL) powdered milk, measuring cups, measuring spoons, large bowl, wooden spoon, wax paper

 Directions: In the bowl, mix the peanut butter, honey, sesame seeds, and powdered milk. Give each child a piece of wax paper with a spoonful of the mixture on it. Tell them to shape the mixture so that it looks like a bird's nest. Then give them some colored mini-marshmallows to put in their nests as bird eggs.

Name: _____ Date: _____

Birds Everywhere

Trace the numbers. Then color each bird a different color.

Name: _____ Date: _____

Match the Birds

Draw lines to match the birds that look alike. Then color the pairs of birds alike.

Name: _____ Date: _____

Nests and Eggs

Trace the numbers on each nest. In the nests, draw the number of eggs that match the numbers. Color the eggs.

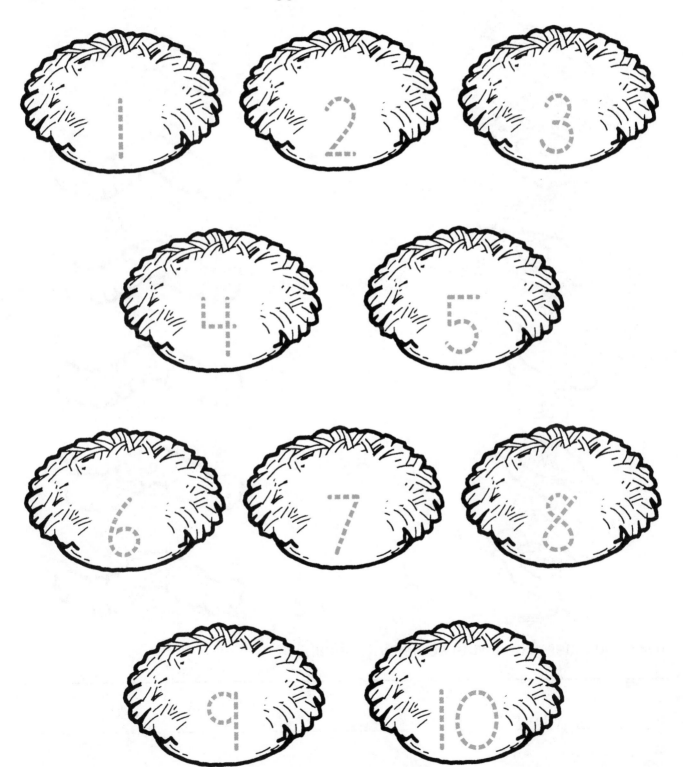

Name: _____ Date: _____

Letter Birds

Draw lines to match the uppercase letters on the birds with the lowercase letters on the worms.

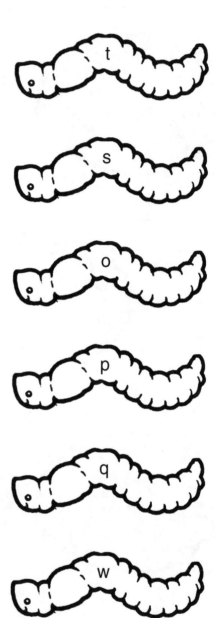

Trace the letter. Then write some by yourself.

May

	Sunday	Monday	Tuesday	Wednesday	Thursday	Friday	Saturday

Sunshine

═══════════════════════════ **DAY 1** ═══════════════════════════

Sharing Time: May is a good time to review important concepts with the children, while continuing to teach them new ones. Start a discussion about the sun and its effects on the Earth. Ask the children to speculate what life would be like without the sun.

Movement Activity: Have students practice "The Sun" (page 223) all week.

Lesson: The Sun Is Shining!

    Materials: markers, copies of page 224

    Directions: Have the children use yellow markers to color the sun and trace its rays. Have them color the ground and tree trunk brown and the rest of the tree green.

═══════════════════════════ **DAY 2** ═══════════════════════════

Sharing Time: Provide students with a variety of books that include pictures of the sun and a simple explanation of how it works.

Lesson: How Many Suns?

    Materials: colored pencils or markers, copies of page 225

    Directions: Have the children count the suns in each box and write the corresponding number. Then have them color all of the suns.

═══════════════════════════ **DAY 3** ═══════════════════════════

Lesson: Sun Letters!

    Materials: crayons, markers, or colored pencils; copies of page 226

    Directions: Have students draw lines to match the uppercase and lowercase letters.

═══════════════════════════ **DAY 4** ═══════════════════════════

Arts and Crafts: Sun

    Materials: 3" (7.5 cm) Styrofoam balls, one per child; yellow spray paint; yellow pipe cleaners; permanent black markers; plastic eyes (optional); glue (optional)

    Directions: The day before doing this activity with students, paint the Styrofoam balls yellow. Be sure that you have one ball for each child. Cut the pipe cleaners in half. Give each child a Styrofoam ball and some pipe cleaner halves. Show the children how to stick the pipe cleaners into the ball to make the sun's rays. Then have students use black markers to draw the sun's facial features. If you prefer, students can glue on plastic eyes and draw the other features.

═══════════════════════════ **DAY 5** ═══════════════════════════

Cooking Experience: Sunshine Salad

    Materials: paper plates, plastic spoons, large container of banana yogurt, raisins, large can of pineapple pieces

    Directions: Put a large spoonful of yogurt on each child's plate. Have the children place the pineapple pieces extending out from the yogurt to look like the sun's rays. Ask them to use the raisins for the facial features.

The Sun

Movement Activity

The sun is big and round.

(Hold hands above head, and make a circle with arms.)

The rays stretch out long.

(Stretch out arms.)

The sun warms the ground, and the plants start to grow.

(Stretch arms upward like plants growing.)

Then the sun will smile.

(Put hands above head, make a circle with arms, and smile.)

Deanna Reynolds

#2594 Treasury of Year–Round Preschool Activities

Name: _____ Date: _____

The Sun Is Shining!

Use yellow to color the sun and trace its rays. Color the ground and the tree trunk brown. Then color the rest of the tree green.

Name: _____ Date: _____

How Many Suns?

Count the suns in each box. Write the number that shows how many suns there are in each box. Then color all of the suns.

Name: _____ Date: _____

Sun Letters!

Draw lines to match the uppercase letters with the lowercase letters.

Z   t   D   f
M   b   N   r
Y   m   F   g
T   z   R   d
B   y   G   n

Planting

DAY 1

Sharing Time: Talk about how plants grow. Point out that plants need minerals from soil, water, and sunlight to live.

Lesson: What a Plant Needs to Grow Book

> **Materials:** crayons, markers, scissors, hole punch, brads, copies of pages 228–230

> **Directions:** Have students color the leaves. Have them cut out the leaves and punch a hole at the top of each. Help them put the pages in order and bind them with a brad.

DAY 2

Lesson: Plant a Seed

> **Materials:** potting soil, Styrofoam cups, seeds, water

> **Directions:** Have the children plant some fast-growing seeds, such as bean or radish seeds. Have them water their seeds and keep them in a sunny place. When the seeds begin to sprout, allow the children to take their plants home to share with their families.

DAY 3

Sharing Time: Read any version of *Jack and the Beanstalk*. Afterwards, discuss which aspects of the story are real and which are imaginary.

Lesson: Make a Beanstalk

> **Materials:** empty paper towel rolls, green tissue paper, green markers or crayons, scissors, glue, dried beans (optional), copies of page 231

> **Directions:** Collect empty paper towel rolls. Have students glue green tissue paper onto the rolls. Then have them color and cut out the leaves on page 231. Tell them to glue the leaves onto the paper towel rolls. Students may wish to glue dried beans onto their stalks.

DAY 4

Sharing Time: Talk about how vegetables can be different sizes—small, medium, and large.

Lesson: Sizes

> **Materials:** crayons, scissors, glue, copies of page 232

> **Directions:** Have students cut out the vegetables and sort them by size — small, medium, large. Tell them to glue each vegetable in the correct box.

DAY 5

Cooking Experience: Dirt Cup with Beans

> **Materials:** plastic cups, plastic spoons, measuring cups, milk, large package of instant chocolate pudding, whipped topping, crushed chocolate sandwich cookies, jellybeans

> **Directions:** Invite the children to help make the pudding. Mix half of the crushed cookies and the whipped topping. Put a little of this mixture in each child's bowl. Then fill the bowls with pudding. Sprinkle a little bit of crushed cookies on top of the pudding. When the children aren't looking, hide 2–3 jellybeans in each child's pudding. Tell children to pretend the pudding and cookies are dirt. Have them search for Jack's magic beans.

Name: _____ Date: _____

What a Plant Needs to Grow

Color the leaves below and on page 229. Cut out the leaves. Punch a hole at the top of each leaf where shown. Then use a brad to make a booklet from the leaves.

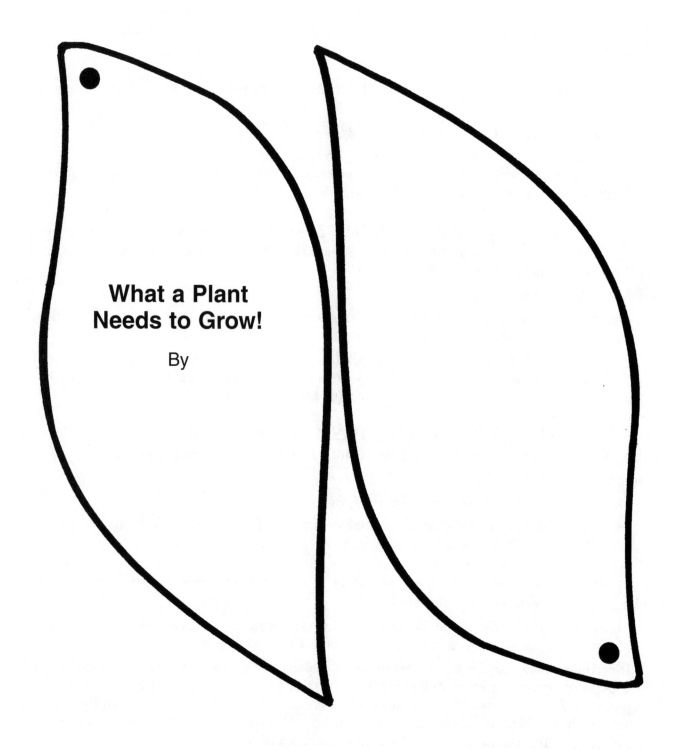

What a Plant Needs to Grow!

By

Name: _____ Date: _____

What a Plant Needs to Grow *(cont.)*

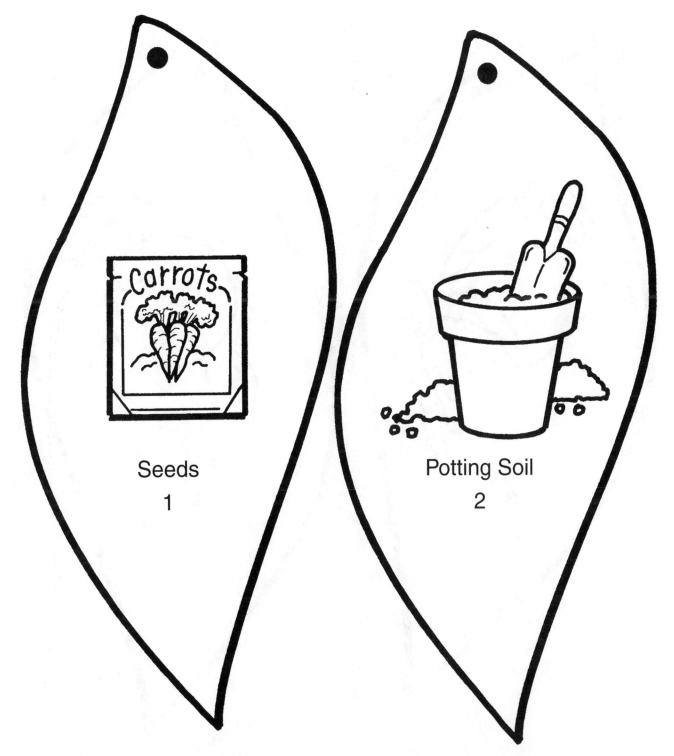

Seeds
1

Potting Soil
2

Name: _____ Date: _____

What a Plant Needs to Grow *(cont.)*

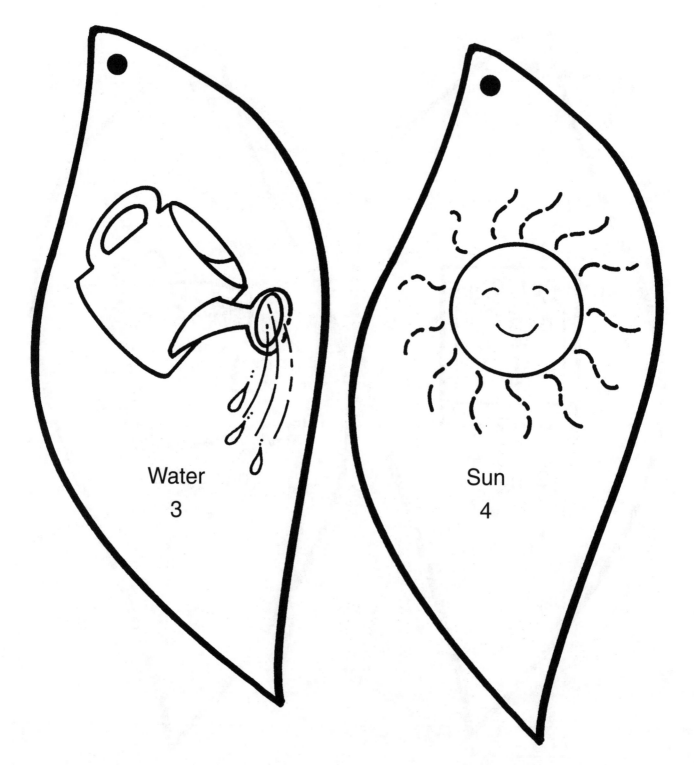

Water
3

Sun
4

Name: _____ Date: _____

Make a Beanstalk

Cover an empty paper towel tube with green tissue paper. Use green crayon or marker to color the leaves shown below. Cut them out. Then glue them onto the paper towel tube.

Name: _____   Date: _____

Sizes

Cut out the vegetables. Sort them by size — small, medium, large. Glue each vegetable in the correct box.

Small	Medium	Large

Growing Fruits and Vegetables

═══════════════ DAY 1 ═══════════════

Sharing Time: Talk about vegetables that grow above and below the ground. Provide a variety of books about fruits, vegetables, and gardening.

Lesson: Fruits and Vegetables

   Materials: markers, copies of page 234

   Directions: Have the children circle the picture in each row that looks like the first picture. You may wish to have the children put their fingers under the first picture in each row to make the comparisons easier for them.

═══════════════ DAY 2 ═══════════════

Sharing Time: Review that vegetables grow above and below the ground. Tell students that fruit also grows in different places, such as on the ground, on vines, and on trees.

Lesson: Growing Fruits and Vegetables

   Materials: colored pencils, crayons, scissors, glue, copies of page 235

   Directions: Color the fruit trees. Color the vegetables. Then cut them out and glue them above or below the ground depending on where they grow in real life.

═══════════════ DAY 3 ═══════════════

Sharing Time: Compare/contrast different fruits and vegetables. Talk about how they look, feel, smell, and taste.

Lesson: Different Fruits and Vegetables

   Materials: colored pencils or markers, copies of page 236

   Directions: In each row, have the children color the picture that is different.

═══════════════ DAY 4 ═══════════════

Sharing Time: Have the children imagine that they are planning a fruit and/or vegetable garden. Ask what they would like to plant and why they made those choices.

Arts and Crafts: Garden Scene

   Materials: magazines, scissors, glue, colored pencils, crayons, construction paper, glitter

   Directions: Have the children make fruit/vegetable garden scenes. They can use magazine pictures or draw to create their scenes.

═══════════════ DAY 5 ═══════════════

Cooking Experience: Vegetable Bites and Dip

   Materials: package of ranch dip mix, bowl, whisk, measuring cup, milk, mayonnaise, paper plates, long wooden skewers, cucumbers, cherry tomatoes, carrots, celery

   Directions: Let the children help make the dip. Then put it aside. Cut up the vegetables into bite-size pieces. Give each child a paper plate, wooden skewer, and some vegetables. Have the children put the vegetables on the skewer and lay it on the plate. Help them pour the dip over the skewer. Caution them not to stab themselves with the skewer when they eat the vegetables.

Name: _____ Date: _____

Fruits and Vegetables

Circle the picture in each row that looks like the first picture.

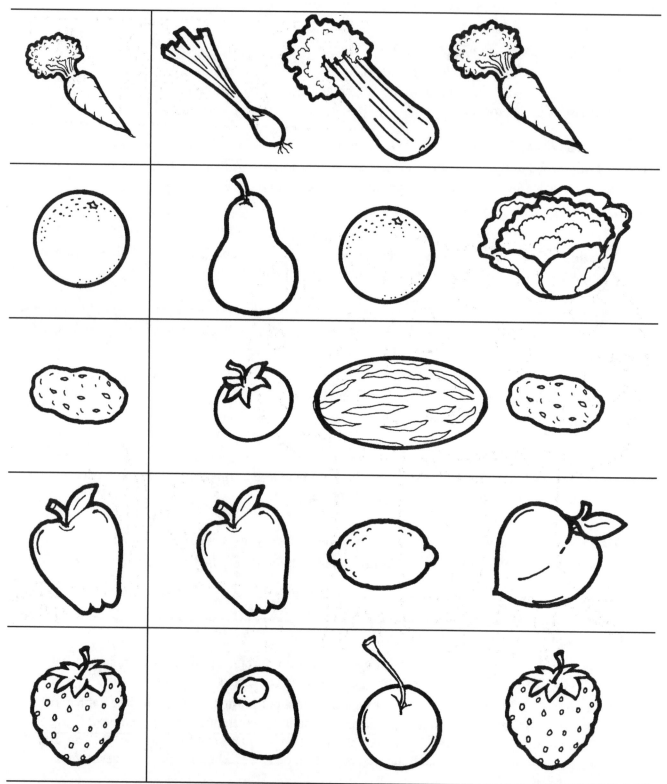

Name: _____ Date: _____

Growing Fruits and Vegetables

Color the fruit trees. Color the vegetables. Then cut them out and glue them above or below the ground depending on where they grow.

Name: _____ Date: _____

Different Fruits and Vegetables

Color the picture that is different in each row.

May Flowers

━━━ DAY 1 ━━━

Sharing Time: Tell the children that flowers grow like other plants. They need minerals from the soil, water, and sunlight to live. Provide a variety of books with pictures of flowers.

Movement Activity: Have students practice "The Flower" (page 238) all week.

Lesson: Mary's Garden

    Materials: crayons, markers, or colored pencils; copies of page 239

    Directions: Have the children color the large flowers red, the medium flowers blue, and the small flowers yellow.

━━━ DAY 2 ━━━

Sharing Time: Ask the children to describe their favorite flowers.

Lesson: The Flowers

    Materials: colored pencils or fine-point markers, copies of page 240

    Directions: Have the children draw lines to match the flowers on the left with the flowers on the right. Then encourage them to color the flowers.

━━━ DAY 3 ━━━

Sharing Time: Talk to the children about fruit that grows on trees. Explain that some flowers on trees change into fruit. Provide some examples such as apples, oranges, and lemons.

Lesson: The Fruit Tree

    Materials: brown crayons, 1" (2.5 cm) squares of green and yellow tissue paper, glue, red tempera paint, aluminum pie pans, copies of page 241

    Directions: Have the children color the tree brown. Then tell them to crush the tissue paper into leaves and flowers. Have the children glue these onto the tree. To make the fruit, have the children dip their index fingers into red tempera paint and make prints on the tree.

━━━ DAY 4 ━━━

Sharing Time: If possible today, visit a plant nursery to see the different kinds of plants that are grown there. Buy some flower seeds that are easy to grow.

    Materials: clay pots or large paper cups, potting soil, flower seeds

    Directions: Let the children plant the seeds in paper cups or clay pots. After the plants begin to grow, have the children take them home to share with their families. These flowers make great Mother's Day gifts. See page 242 for additional Mother's Day ideas.

━━━ DAY 5 ━━━

Cooking Experience: Fruit Flowers

    Materials: paper plates, plastic knives, string licorice, strawberries, bananas, kiwi

    Directions: Let the children cut the strawberries and kiwi in half and then into thin slices. Give each child a banana slice. Have them use the banana slice for the flower's center, the strawberry slices for the petals, and the licorice for the stem. Then have them place two slices of kiwi next to the licorice for the leaves.

The Flower

Movement Activity

Plant a seed in the ground.

(Index finger tapping on palm of other hand.)

Water the seed and watch.

(Pretend to water the palm of hand.)

Let the sun shine on it.

(Put hands above head and make a circle with arms.)

Watch as the plant pops out of the ground and

unfolds into a beautiful flower.

(Cup both hands.)

Deanna Reynolds

Name: _____ Date: _____

Mary's Garden

Mary has many flowers in her garden.

Color the large flowers red.

Color the medium flowers blue.

Color the small flowers yellow.

Name: _____　Date: _____

The Flowers

Draw lines to match the flowers on the left with the flowers on the right. Then color the flowers.

Name: _____ Date: _____

The Fruit Tree

Color the tree brown. Then add leaves, flowers, and fruit.

Mother's Day

For Mother's Day, which is in May, have the children make something for their mothers. Feel free to use the following suggestions or any of your own ideas.

Tissue Flowers and Vase

Materials: 6–10" (15–25 cm) tissue paper circles, various colors; spray paint; green pipe cleaners; 6–8" (15–20 cm) small necked bottles; scissors

Directions: Spray paint the bottle gold, or ask the children to name one or two of their favorite colors and use those to spray paint the bottles. Next, have the children pick 3 to 5 tissue paper circles that are different colors. Have them place the pieces of tissue paper on top of each other and pull these down in the middle about 1" (2.5 cm). Show them how to push a green pipe cleaner through the part that they pulled down and twist it until it is tight. Tell them to fan out the tissue paper to make it look like a flower. Have the children place their flowers in their vases.

Clay Pot and Plant

Materials: 2" (5 cm) green house plants; 6" (15 cm) clay pots; paint, various colors; paintbrushes; spray clay sealer; potting soil; old shirts, smocks, or plastic painting aprons

Directions: Let the children paint the pots different colors. After the paint dries, spray the pots with a sealer. Allow the pots to dry overnight. Next have the children help pour potting soil into the pot and plant the greenhouse plant.

Personalized Magnet

Materials: wooden shapes, such as hearts and stars; paint, various colors; paintbrushes; glossy sealer; close-up picture of each child; magnets; hot glue gun

Directions: Trim the photographs so they will fit on the wooden shapes. Let the children paint the shapes. After the paint has dried, spray the shapes with a glossy sealer. Allow the sealer to dry overnight. Use a hot glue gun to attach a magnet onto the back of each wooden shape. Then have the children glue their trimmed pictures onto the front of the wooden shapes.

June

Sunday	Monday	Tuesday	Wednesday	Thursday	Friday	Saturday

Vacations and Transportation

DAY 1

Sharing Time: Discuss the many ways people travel from place to place in their daily lives and when they are on vacation. Ask students to brainstorm modes of transportation.

Lesson: What's Missing?

> **Materials:** colored pencils, crayons, or markers, copies of page 245

> **Directions:** Have the children fill in the missing parts to make the bottom car look like the top car.

DAY 2

Sharing Time: Take the class to the library to check out books about transportation. In addition, have students tell about places they have visited and how they got to and from those locations.

Lesson: Ways to Travel

> **Materials:** colored pencils, copies of page 246

> **Directions:** Have the children draw lines to match the pictures on the left with the pictures on the right.

DAY 3

Lesson: Time to Travel

> **Materials:** markers or colored pencils, copies of page 247

> **Directions:** Have the children draw a line to show how the airplane can get to the castle. Point out that there is only one route that the airplane can travel.

DAY 4

Arts and Crafts: Sailboat Race

> **Materials:** extra wide craft sticks, small white construction paper triangles, toothpicks, markers, glue, hot glue gun, wading pool (optional)

> **Directions:** Have each child make a boat using a craft stick for the bottom, a toothpick for the mast, and a triangle for the sail. Have them color the craft stick and sail. Use a hot glue gun to put the pieces together. If possible, provide a wading pool filled with water and have the children blow their sailboats to race them across the pool.

DAY 5

Cooking Experience: Peanut Butter Airplanes

> **Materials:** ½ cup (120 mL) peanut butter, 2 tablespoons (30 mL) honey, 2 tablespoons (30 mL) sesame seeds, ⅓ cup (80 mL) powdered milk, sliced almonds, raisins, measuring cups, measuring spoons, large bowl, wooden spoon, wax paper

> **Directions:** In the bowl, mix the peanut butter, honey, sesame seeds, and powdered milk. Give each child a square of wax paper with a small spoonful of the mixture. Let the children shape the mixture into the body of an airplane. Use raisins for the windows, thinly sliced apple for the wings and fantail, and almond slivers for the propellers.

Name: _____ Date: _____

What's Missing?

Fill in the missing parts to make the bottom car look like the top car.

Name: _____ Date: _____

Ways to Travel

Draw lines to match the pictures on the left with the pictures on the right.

Name: _____   Date: _____

Time to Travel

Draw a line to show how the airplane can get to the castle.

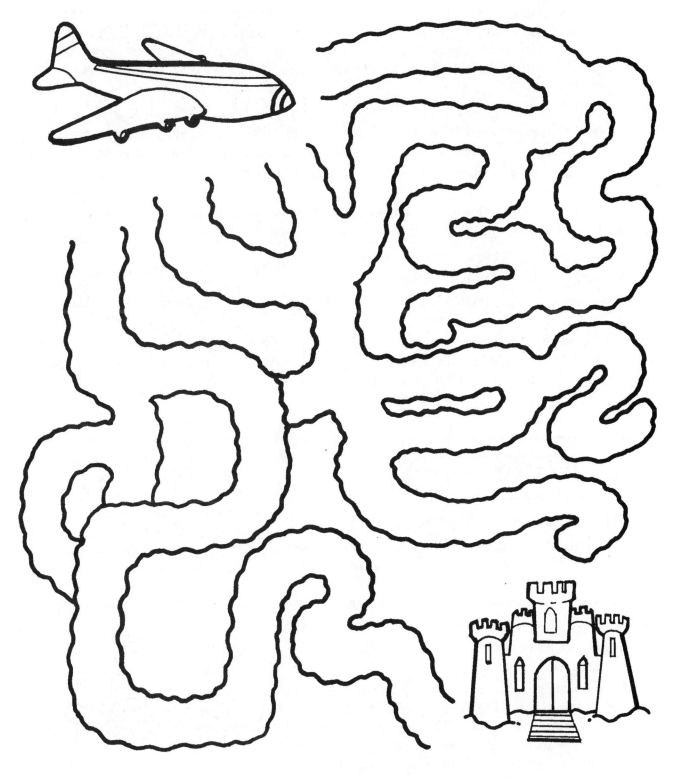

Germany

The next three week's lessons focus on the countries of Germany, Mexico, and Japan. You may wish to introduce the children to other countries as well.

DAY 1

Sharing Time: Share books with pictures of Germany and the German flag with the children. Tell students that when children in Germany go to school for the first time, they are given a large cone made out of paper. The parents decorate the cone. Then it is filled with tasty snacks for the first day of school.

Lesson: German Cornucopia

    Materials: markers; crayons; wrapping paper; stickers; glitter; fabric; glue; tagboard; scissors; snacks, such as nuts, raisins, and/or cookies; cellophane tape; stapler; copies of page 249

    Directions: Help the children follow the directions on page 249 to make a cornucopia.

DAY 2

Sharing Time: Read and discuss any version of the story *Hansel and Gretel*.

Lesson: Hansel and Gretel Find Their Way Home

    Materials: colored pencils, copies of page 250

    Directions: Have the children draw a line to show Hansel and Gretel the way home.

DAY 3

Sharing Time: Take a field trip to a wooded area, park, or playground. Have the children pretend to be either Hansel or Gretel and act out the story. You may wish to drop breadcrumbs on the way back to the classroom. If you do, the birds will love it.

DAY 4

Sharing Time: Compare/contrast the things that Hansel and Gretel saw in the forest with what the children saw on their field trip.

Lesson: What Hansel and Gretel Saw!

    Materials: copies of page 251

    Directions: Have the children draw a picture of something they saw on the field trip. Ask them to dictate a story about their pictures as you write it.

DAY 5

Cooking Experience: Gingerbread Houses

    Materials: paper plates, plastic knives, graham crackers, white icing, gumdrops and other candies

    Directions: Have each child assemble a small gingerbread house using two full graham crackers for two walls, two half graham crackers for the other two walls, and a full cracker for a flat roof. If the children are able, they can use two half graham crackers to make a pitched roof. Use the icing to stick the house together and attach the candies.

Name: _____   Date: _____

German Cornucopia

Cut out the pattern shown below. Glue it onto a piece of tagboard. Allow the glue to dry. Then cut out the pattern again. Decorate your cone with crayons, markers, wrapping paper, stickers, glitter, fabric, or anything else you like. Carefully roll the tagboard into the shape of a cone. Tape the cone in place. Cut a strip of tagboard to use as a handle. Be sure it is long enough before you put it on the cone. Then staple it in place.

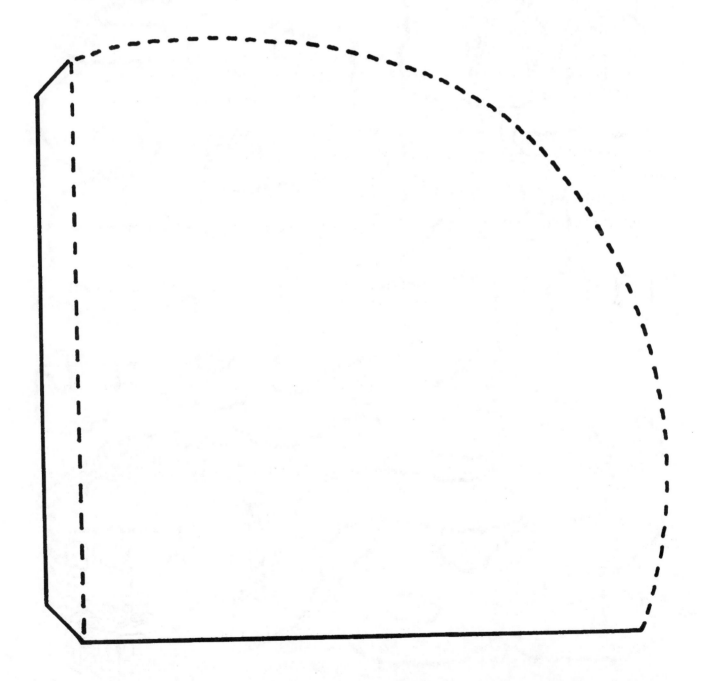

Name: _____   Date: _____

Hansel and Gretel Find Their Way Home

Draw a line to show Hansel and Gretel the way to their home.

Name: _____ Date: _____

What Hansel and Gretel Saw!

Draw a picture of something you saw on the field trip. Tell about your picture.

Mexico

═══════════════════════ **DAY 1** ═══════════════════════

Sharing Time: Share books and pictures of Mexico and the Mexican flag with the children. Talk about what children in Mexico do for fun and the celebrations they have.

Lesson: Break a Piñata

   Materials: colored pencils, markers, glue (optional), glitter (optional), copies of page 253

   Directions: Have the children color the picture. You may wish to let them use glitter on their pictures.

═══════════════════════ **DAY 2** ═══════════════════════

Sharing Time: Talk about different kinds of piñatas.

Lesson: Piñatas that Match

   Materials: colored pencils or markers, copies of page 254

   Directions: Have the children draw lines to match the piñatas on the right with the piñatas on the left. Tell them to color the matching pairs of piñatas the same.

═══════════════════════ **DAY 3** ═══════════════════════

Sharing Time: Tell the children that they are going to prepare for a piñata party.

Lesson: Mosaic Mask

   Materials: small pieces of construction paper or tissue paper, various colors; glue; scissors; thin elastic; stapler; copies of page 255

   Directions: Have the children cut out the mask and the eyes, nose, and mouth. Have them glue on pieces of colored tissue paper or construction paper to decorate the mask. Then measure each child's mask against his/her face and staple a length of elastic to both sides of the mask. Make sure the elastic is tight enough to keep the mask on the child's face but loose enough so that it isn't uncomfortable.

═══════════════════════ **DAY 4** ═══════════════════════

Sharing Time: Have a piñata party. Ahead of time, stuff a piñata with treats for the children and hang it from a tree or other suitable location. If possible, during the party play music from Mexico. Have the children wear their masks (page 255) for a parade around the school. At the end of the party, let them take turns using a stick to hit the piñata until it breaks.

═══════════════════════ **DAY 5** ═══════════════════════

Cooking Experience: Quesadillas (Mexican pizza)

   Materials: cookie sheet, paper plates, tortillas, shredded cheese, sliced black olives, chopped tomatoes, mild salsa (optional)

   Directions: Preheat the oven to 350 degrees Fahrenheit (175 degrees Celsius). Put the tortillas on the cookie sheet. Let each child choose the toppings (cheese, olives, tomatoes, salsa) for the tortilla. Heat the tortillas in the oven for 5–7 minutes or until the cheese melts. Allow the quesadillas to cool before serving.

Name: _____ Date: _____

Break a Piñata

These children are having fun breaking a piñata. Color the picture.

Name: _____ Date: _____

Piñatas that Match

Draw lines to match the piñatas on the right with the piñatas on the left. Color
the matching pairs of piñatas the same.

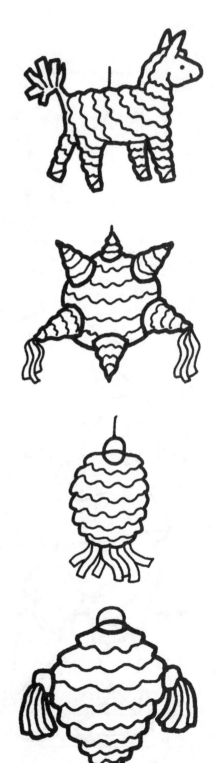

Name: _____ Date: _____

Mosaic Mask

Cut out the mask. Then cut out the eyes, nose, and mouth. Glue on pieces of colored tissue paper or construction paper to decorate the mask.

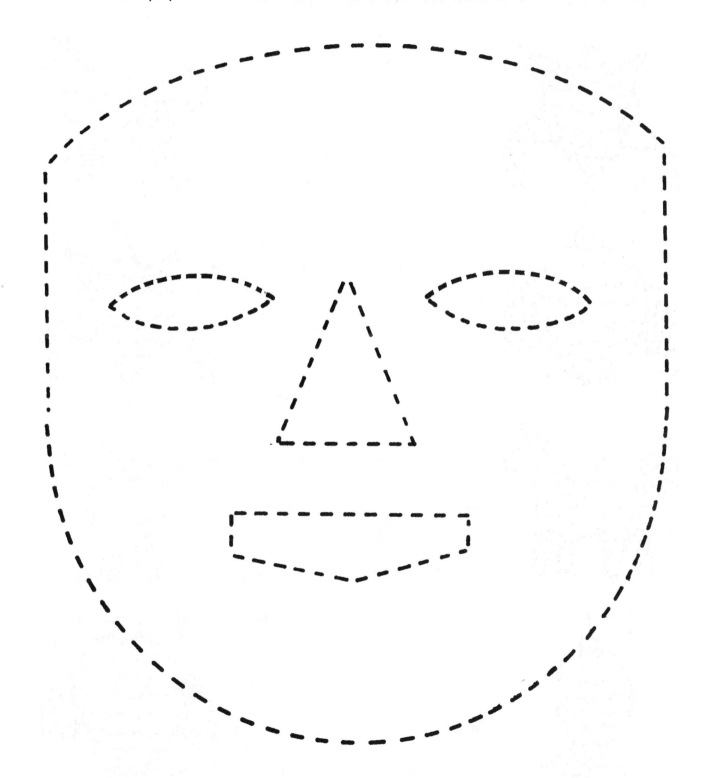

Japan

DAY 1

Sharing Time: Share books with pictures of Japan and the Japanese flag with the children. Point out that Japan is a group of islands. Describe some of Japan's beautiful celebrations.

Lesson: Flags

> **Materials:** colored pencils, copies of page 257
>
> **Directions:** Have the children draw lines to match the flags on the left with the flags on the right. You may wish to review which flag goes with which country. On the back of the paper, ask them to draw and color their own flags.

DAY 2

Sharing Time: Describe or show pictures of some decorations used in Japanese celebrations.

Lesson: Japanese Lantern

> **Materials:** watercolors, glue, scissors, 2" (5 cm)-wide strip of construction paper, copies of page 258
>
> **Directions:** Have the children paint the lantern using watercolors. Allow the paint to dry. Then have the children cut along the dotted lines. Show them how to glue Tab A to Tab B.

DAY 3

Sharing Time: Tell students about the Children's Festival and how Japanese children like to make kites for this celebration. If possible, have students take turns flying a kite.

Arts and Crafts: Make a Kite

> **Materials:** 9" x 12" (22.5 x 30 cm) white construction paper; crayons; markers; glue; scissors; glitter; crepe paper streamers, various colors
>
> **Directions:** This kite is just for decoration. It will not fly. Draw diamond shapes on the construction paper, making one for each child. Let the children decorate and cut out the kites. Next let them use crepe paper streamers for the tail of the kite.

DAY 4

Sharing Time: Discuss Japanese gardens.

Lesson: Cherry Blossom Tree

> **Materials:** plastic cups; plaster of Paris; tree branches; pink, purple, and white 2" (5 cm) tissue paper squares; glue
>
> **Directions:** Before the children arrive, place small tree branches in cups filled with plaster of Paris. Be sure you have one for each child. Once the plaster dries, have the children make cherry blossoms from the tissue paper squares and glue them onto the tree branches.

DAY 5

Cooking Experience: Rice Cakes

> **Materials:** paper plates; plastic knives; rice cakes, various flavors; peanut butter; jelly; thinly sliced fruit
>
> **Directions:** Let the children choose what they want to put on top of their rice cakes.

Name: _____ Date: _____

Flags

Draw lines to match the flags on the left with the flags on the right. On the back of this paper, draw and color your own flag.

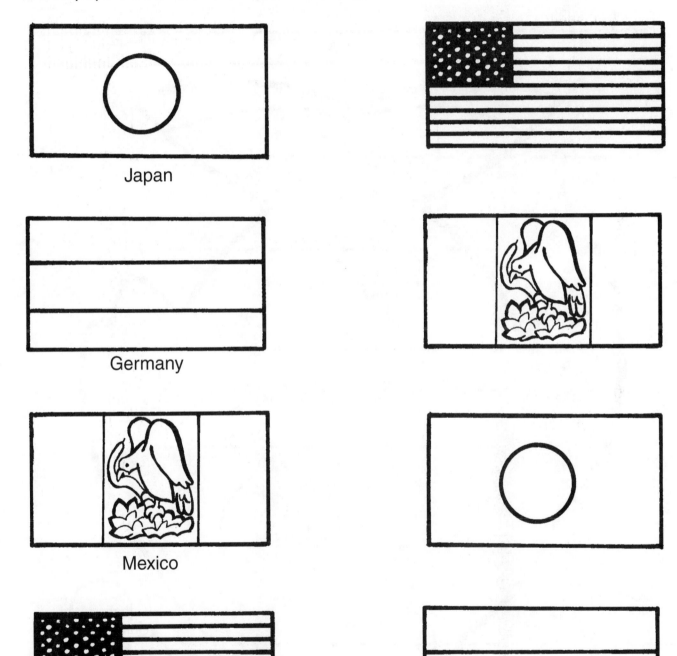

Japan

Germany

Mexico

U.S.A.

Name: _____ Date: _____

Japanese Lantern

Paint the lantern using watercolors. Allow the paint to dry. Then cut along the dotted lines. Glue Tab A to Tab B.

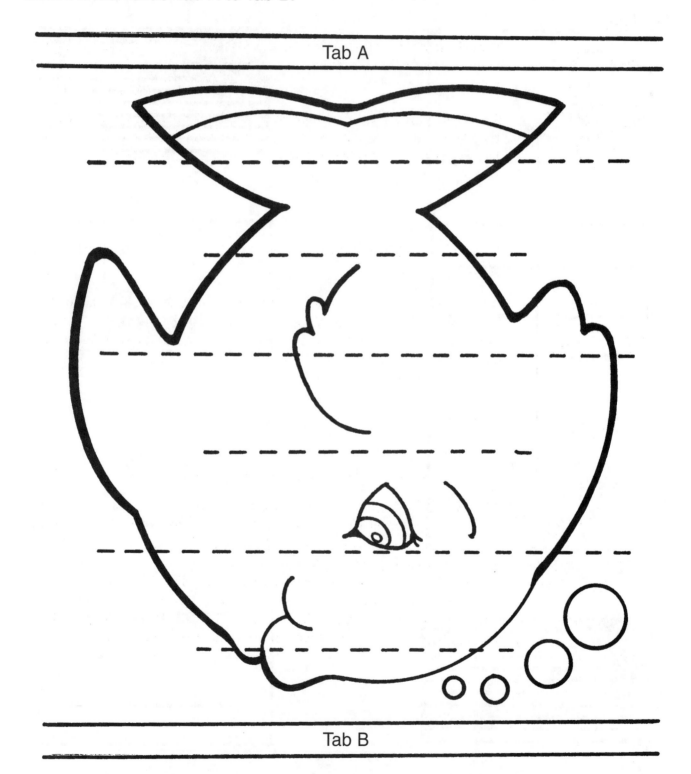

Tab A

Tab B

Father's Day

For Father's Day, which is in June, have the children make something for their fathers. Feel free to use the following suggestions or any of your own ideas.

Key Ring

Materials: 1" (2.5 cm) wooden shape, such as hearts or stars; spray sealer; paints, various colors; paintbrushes, key rings (available at craft stores); ice pick

Directions: Use the ice pick to punch a small hole in each wooden shape. Then let the children paint the shape. Let the paint dry overnight. The next day, spray the wooden shapes with a glossy sealer. Put a key ring through the hole in each wooden shape.

Paperweight

Materials: felt; rocks; glue; nuts; bolts; washers; spray paint, various colors including gold and silver

Directions: Have the children collect fist-sized rocks or bring some to class. Have the children glue a piece of felt onto the bottom of the rock. Then let them glue on different sizes of nuts, bolts, or washers to make a design or a face. After the glue dries, spray paint the whole paperweight gold, silver, or the child's favorite color. Allow the paint to dry overnight.

Pencil Holder

Materials: large baby food jars; permanent markers, various colors; felt; hot glue gun; glue; black marker; pens and/or pencils (optional)

Directions: Give each child a baby food jar. Tell them to draw designs or pictures using the permanent markers. Let the ink dry overnight. Use a hot glue gun to attach a piece of felt to the bottom of each jar. Have the children decide what kind of greeting they want to write on the pencil holder. Examples: Dad's Pencils or Daddy's Things. Use a black marker to write what the children request. You may want to enlist the help of parent volunteers or older students to help with this activity. If possible, provide pens and/or pencils for the children to put in their pencil holders.

July

Sunday	Monday	Tuesday	Wednesday	Thursday	Friday	Saturday

Fourth of July and Fireworks

═══ DAY 1 ═══

Sharing Time: Ask students what kind of summertime activities they enjoy doing.

Movement Activity: Have students practice "Fireworks" (page 262) all week.

Lesson: Summertime Food

> **Materials:** crayons or markers, copies of page 263

> **Directions:** Review the numbers 1-5. Explain how to color according to the numbers.

═══ DAY 2 ═══

Sharing Time: Discuss picnics and what kinds of food the children like to eat while on picnics. In addition, ask the children when and where they have ever seen fireworks.

Lesson: Picnic Day

> **Materials:** magazines with food pictures, glue, scissors, crayons, copies of page 264

> **Directions:** Have the children color the picnic blanket. Tell them to find pictures of their favorite foods in magazines. Have them cut out the pictures and glue them onto the blanket.

═══ DAY 3 ═══

Sharing Time: Discuss thing that people can do to stay safe while working or playing in the sun.

Lesson: Summer Fun Visor

> **Materials:** cardstock, watercolors, glue, scissors, copies of page 265

> **Directions:** Help the children follow the directions on page 265.

═══ DAY 4 ═══

Sharing Time: Have a Fourth of July Parade. This activity can be done on the weekday that is closest to the Fourth of July. Have the children wear their sun visors (page 265). Let them march and play music for the parade. Invite parents to come and watch their children. Serve snacks, such as watermelon or ice cream.

═══ DAY 5 ═══

Cooking Experience: Fourth of July Kabobs

> **Warning:** Caution children not to stab themselves on the skewers when eating these kabobs.

> *Option 1* — **Materials:** BBQ grill, metal skewers, hot dogs cut into 2" (5 cm) slices, bell peppers or other vegetables

> **Directions:** Help the children put the hot dogs and vegetables onto the metal skewers. Cook them over the grill. Allow them to cool. Then serve.

> *Option 2* — **Materials:** wooden skewers; bite-size pieces of cucumbers, carrots, celery, tomatoes, etc., and/or bite-size pieces of bananas, strawberries, grapes, kiwi, etc.; ranch and/or yogurt dip

> **Directions:** Have the children put fruit and/or vegetables on wooden skewers and let them dip the kabobs into either ranch dip and/or yogurt dip.

Fireworks
Movement Activity

Fireworks, fireworks popping here and there in the sky.

(Hold hand to forehead and pretend to look at sky.)

Fireworks, fireworks going pop, pop, pop.

(Say "pop, pop, pop" loudly.)

Fireworks, fireworks going bang, bang, bang.

(Clap loudly three times.)

Fireworks, fireworks going pop, bang, pop, bang, pop, bang!

(Say the pops loudly and clap loudly for each bang.)

Alysha Reynolds

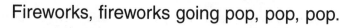
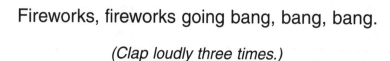

Name: _____ Date: _____

Summertime Food

Color the 1s brown.

Color the 2s yellow.

Color the 3s pink.

Color the 4s green.

Color the 5s red.

Color the 6s black.

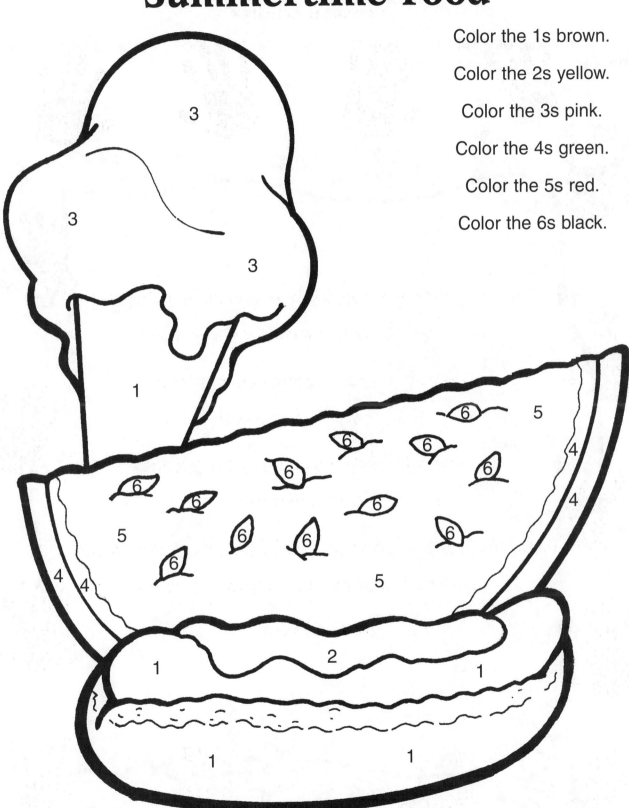

Name: _____ Date: _____

Picnic Day

Color the picnic blanket. Find pictures of your favorite foods in magazines. Cut them out and glue them onto the blanket.

Name: _____ Date: _____

Summer Fun Visor

Paint the visor using watercolors. Allow the paint to dry. Cut out the visor. Then smear glue on the decorations drawn on the visor. Sprinkle glitter onto the glue. Allow the glue to dry. Shake off any extra glitter. Punch holes in the ends of the visor. Then tie a string to the holes. Wear your visor.

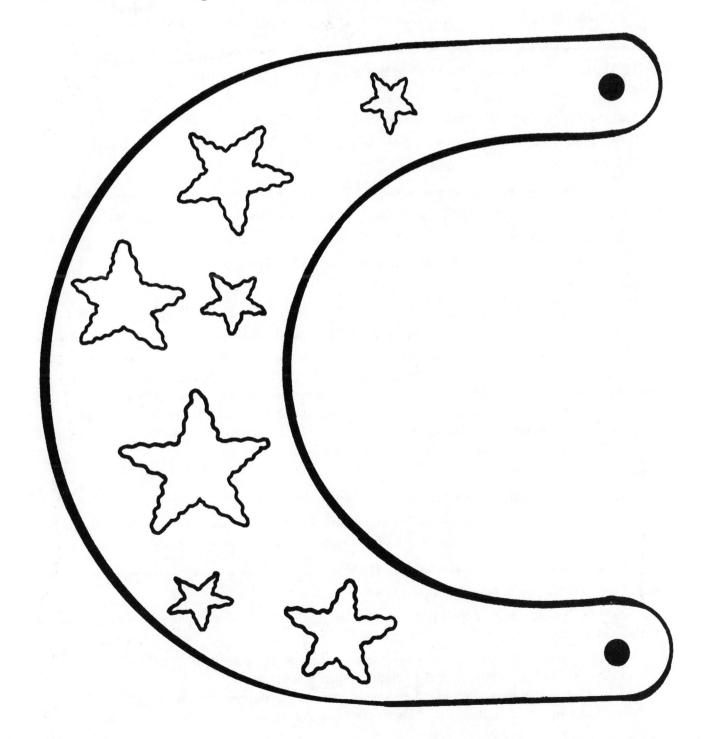

Beaches and Seashells

DAY 1

Sharing Time: This week talk about the beach and seashells. Show students pictures of the different kinds of seashells there are.

Lesson: Counting Seashells

    Materials: colored pencils or markers, copies of page 267

    Directions: Have the children color the correct number of seashells in each row.

DAY 2

Sharing Time: Tell the children that some people keep pet fish in fishbowls or tanks.

Lesson: Fishbowl

    Materials: colored pencils, markers, crayons, scissors, glue, copies of page 268

    Directions: Have the children create their own fishbowls by cutting out the fish and seashells and gluing them in the bowl. Then have them color the picture.

DAY 3

Sharing Time: Have the children tell about experiences with the beach and finding seashells.

Lesson: Finding Seashells

    Materials: colored pencils, crayons or markers, copies of page 269

    Directions: Have the children find 10 seashells that are hidden in the picture. Ask them to color the seashells purple. They can choose any colors for the rest of the picture.

DAY 4

Sharing Time: Invite the children to wear their swimsuits to school. Tell them to bring towels and a change of clothes. If possible, arrange with parent volunteers to take the children to a beach. If this is not possible, make a beach at school. To do so, provide some wading pools filled with water or run some sprinklers in a grassy area. Use a sandbox or a large cardboard box filled with sand to hide seashells for the children to find. *Warning:* Make sure you have enough parent volunteers to watch the children, whether you visit a real beach or create one at school.

Arts and Crafts: Seashell bracelet

    Materials: clear fishing line, beads, seashells and scissors

    Directions: Have students string beads and/or seashells on fishing line. Tie the bracelet around the child's wrist, making sure that it is loose enough for the child to slip on and off.

DAY 5

Cooking Experience: Gelatin Aquarium

    Materials: plastic dessert cups, plastic spoons, large bowl, measuring cups, large spoon, large package of berry blue gelatin, gummy fish

    Directions: Follow the instructions on the gelatin package and pour it into the dessert cups. Refrigerate the gelatin. When it starts to set, add the gummy fish so it looks like they are swimming. Refrigerate the gelatin until it is completely set. Then serve it to the students.

Name: _____ Date: _____

Counting Seashells

Color the correct number of seashells in each row.

3	
5	
1	
9	
10	
6	
2	
8	
4	
7	

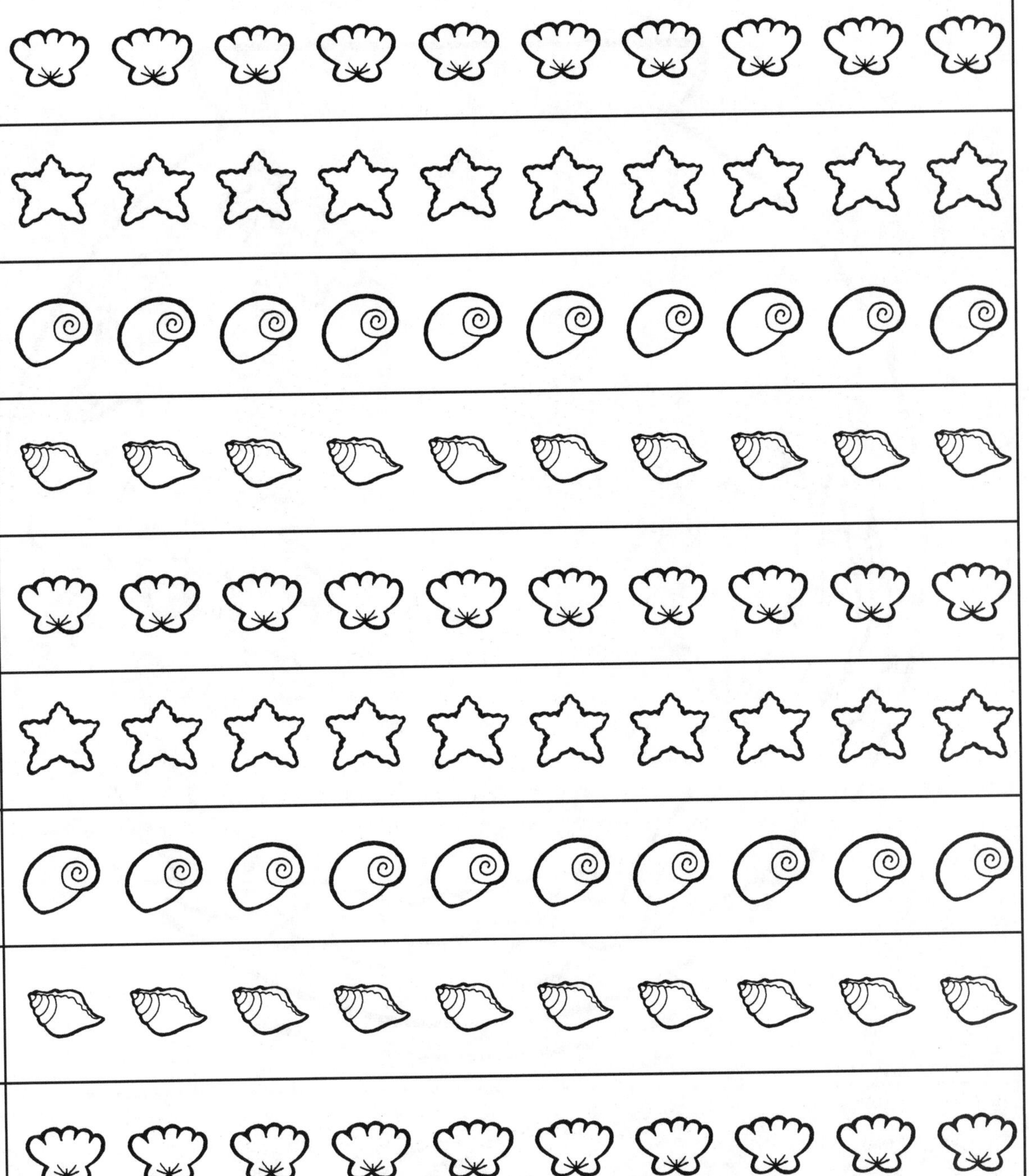

Name: _____ Date: _____

Fishbowl

Cut out the fish and seashells at the bottom of the page. Glue them in the fishbowl. Then color the picture.

Name: _____   Date: _____

Finding Seashells

Find 10 seashells that are hidden in the picture. Color them purple. Then color the rest of the picture.

Starfish and Sand Castles

DAY 1

Sharing Time: Talk to the children about finding starfish in the ocean. Share starfish books and pictures with them.

Lesson: Matching Starfish

Materials: crayons, copies of page 271

Directions: Have the children find the two starfish that have the same number on them. Color these two starfish orange. Color all the other starfish green.

DAY 2

Sharing Time: Talk more about the starfish and how they feel. If possible, have some starfish for the children to touch. Craft and teacher supply stores often carry them. Allow the children to compare/contrast the texture of starfish with some shells.

Lesson: My Starfish

Materials: ½ sheet of coarse sandpaper per child crayons, copies of page 272

Directions: Give each child ½ sheet of coarse sandpaper and crayons. Have them place the sandpaper under the starfish pattern and use a crayon to color it. As an alternative give students glue and colored sand to cover the starfish pattern.

DAY 3

Sharing Time: Have a Sand Castles Day. If you have a sandbox, get it wet so the children can build sand castles. Supply the children with buckets, shovels, and cups. If a sandbox is not available, use a large plastic tub or tubs filled with sand.

DAY 4

Lesson: Sand Castle and Starfish Mobile

Materials: poster board, various colors; yarn; hole punch; scissors; stapler; crayons or watercolors; paintbrushes; copies of page 273

Directions: Directions for the mobile frame appear on page 129. Have the children color and cut out the sand castles and starfish. Help them punch holes where indicated. Have them string a piece of yarn through each hole and attach it to the mobile frame.

DAY 5

Cooking Experience: Sandcups

Materials: plastic dessert cups, plastic spoons, large bowl, spoon, measuring cups, large package of vanilla pudding, milk, ½ box of crushed vanilla wafers

Directions: Have the children help make the pudding. Place some of the crushed vanilla wafers in the bottom of each cup. Then fill the cups with the pudding. Sprinkle the rest of the vanilla wafers on top of the pudding.

Name: _____ Date: _____

Matching Starfish

Find the two starfish that have the same number on them. Color these two starfish orange. Color all the other starfish green.

Name: _____ Date: _____

My Starfish

Name: _____ Date: _____

Sand Castle and Starfish Mobile

Color and cut out the sand castles and starfish. Cut out all the pieces. Punch holes where shown. String a piece of yarn through each hole. Then attach it to the mobile frame.

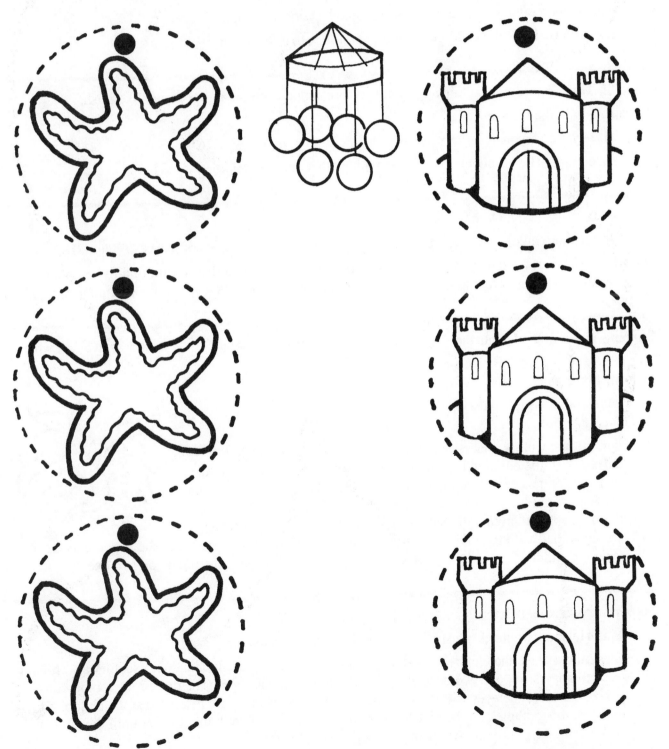

Ocean Life

DAY 1

Sharing Time: During this week, talk about ocean life. Have books and pictures to show the children the kinds of things that live in the ocean, such as octopus, lobsters, fish, starfish, whales, and dolphins.

Lesson: Fishing in the Ocean

> **Materials:** crayons, markers or colored pencils, copies of page 275

> **Directions:** Have the children color all the things that they would find living in the ocean.

DAY 2

Sharing Time: Discuss what kinds of things are not supposed to be in the ocean, like trash.

Lesson: Not in the Ocean

> **Materials:** crayons, markers or colored pencils, copies of page 276

> **Directions:** Have students color all the things that are not supposed to be in the ocean.

DAY 3

Lesson: Sea Life in the Ocean

> **Materials:** crayons, markers, colored pencils, scissors, glue, copies of pages 277 and 278

> **Directions:** Have the children color the things on page 277 that they would find living in the ocean. Tell them to cut these things out and glue them under the water in the ocean on page 278.

DAY 4

Sharing Time: Tell students that an octopus has eight arms. Tell where these creatures live and what they eat.

Lesson: Make an Octopus

> **Materials:** tissue paper, various colors; rubber bands; plastic eyes; scissors; glue

> **Directions:** Cut the pieces of tissue paper in half. Give each child two halves. Tell the children to crumple one piece of tissue paper into a ball and set it aside. Have them take the other piece and lay it out flat. Have them put the crumpled ball in the center. Show them how to pull the flat paper all around the ball using a rubber band. Go over the crumpled ball with the rubber band until it is tight. Be careful since the tissue paper tears easily. Help the children cut eight tentacles for the octopus. Then have them glue on two eyes.

DAY 5

Cooking Experience: Octopus

> **Materials:** paper plates, plastic knives, hot dogs, toothpicks, pan

> **Directions:** Have the children cut slits two-thirds of the way up the hot dog. Next let the children use a toothpick to poke two deep eyes near the top of the hot dog. The deeper the toothpick is poked, the more the eyes will show up after the hot dog is cooked. Be sure that the children do not stick the toothpick all the way through the hot dog. Cook in boiling water until the cut slits curl up and the eyes pop. Allow the hot dogs to cool before serving.

Name: _____ Date: _____

Fishing in the Ocean

Color all the things that you would find living underwater in the ocean.

Name: _____ Date: _____

Not in the Ocean

Color all the things that are not supposed to be in the ocean.

Name: _____ Date: _____

Sea Life in the Ocean

Color the things that you would find living underwater in the ocean. Cut them out and glue them under the water in the ocean on page 278.

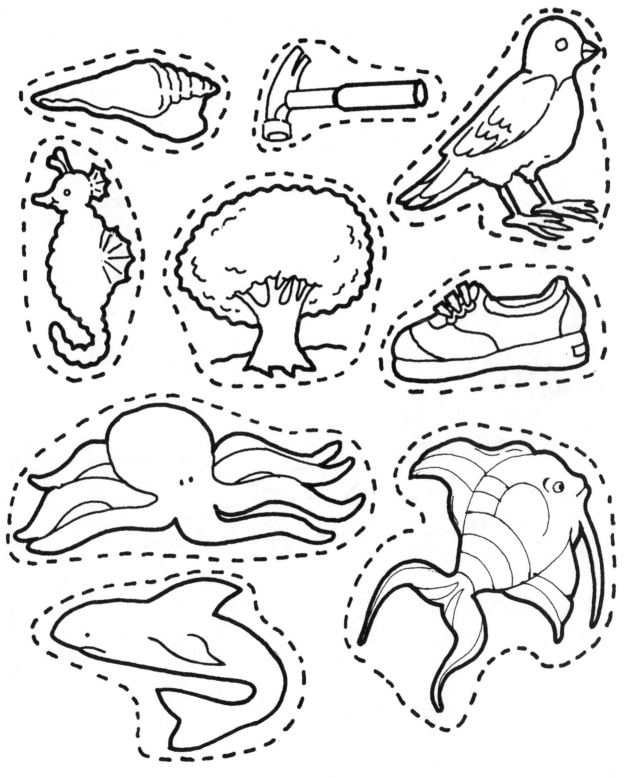

Name: _____ Date: _____

Sea Life in the Ocean *(cont.)*

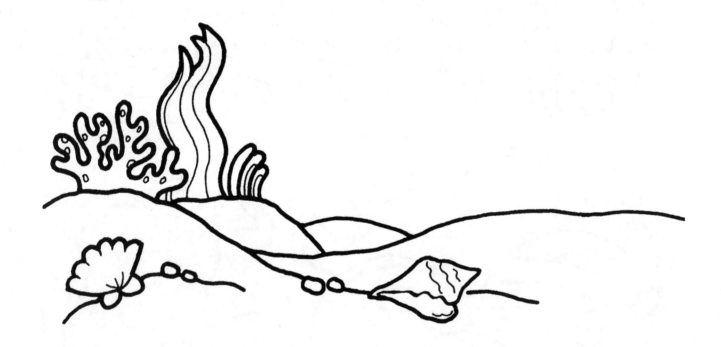

Fish

═══ DAY 1 ═══

Sharing Time: Start this week talking about different kinds, colors, and sizes of fish. Share books about fish with the children. Tell how fish live in rivers, lakes, oceans, aquariums, and fishbowls.

Movement Activity: Have the children practice "I Caught a Fish Alive" (page 281) all week.

Science Experiment: The Dancing Fish

> **Materials:** quart (liter) jar filled with water, measuring cups, measuring spoons, raisins, ⅓ cup (80 mL) white vinegar, 2 teaspoons (10 mL) baking soda

> **Directions:** Fill the jar with water. Gently stir in the white vinegar and baking soda. Then add some raisins to be the fish. At first, the "fish" will sink. However, after a little time they will begin to rise and move around. They will sink and rise for a few hours.

Lesson: Sizes of Fish

> **Materials:** crayons or markers, copies of page 282

> **Directions:** Have the children color the large fish orange, the medium fish blue, and the small fish red.

═══ DAY 2 ═══

Lesson: Fish Suncatcher

> **Materials:** pre-cut two each per child of the fish pattern from clear contact paper, different colors of tissue paper, scissors, yarn and a hole punch, copies of page 283

> **Directions:** For each child, cut two matching fish patterns from the contact paper. Have the children peel the backing off the contact paper and lay both pieces with the sticky side up. Tell them to put small pieces of tissue paper on one piece of contact paper. Have them place the other piece of contact paper on top with the sticky sides together. Help the children seal the edges. Next, have the children punch a hole close to the edge. String a piece of yarn through the hole and hang the suncatcher in a window.

Fish *(cont.)*

DAY 3

Sharing Time: For a snack or treat serve crackers shaped like fish and a blue drink mix.

Lesson: Fill the Aquarium

    Materials: crayons, colored pencils, markers, scissors, glue, copies of page 284

    Directions: Have the children count and color 10 of the fish shown at the bottom of the page. Tell them to cut out those ten fish and glue them in the aquarium.

DAY 4

Sharing Time: Have a Fun and Fish Day. If possible, provide a wading pool filled with water. Have plastic magnetic fish in it. Then let the children use a small magnetic fishing pole to catch some of the fish.

Games:

Crab Walk — Divide the class into two groups. Use colored plastic tape or chalk to mark a start and finish line. Have the children race on their hands and feet like a crab until everyone has had a turn.

Snail Race — Divide the class into two groups. Do this race the same as the Crab Walk, except have the children go very slowly like a snail.

Leap Frog — Divide the class into two groups. Have the children race by squatting down and leaping like frogs. In addition, they may want to croak like frogs.

DAY 5

Cooking Experience: Frosted Fish

    Materials: pre-made cupcakes; paper plates; plastic knives; vanilla frosting; fruit-flavored, o-shaped cereal; colored sugar wafer cookies

    Directions: Have the children frost their cupcakes with the white icing. Tell them to use the fruit-flavored, o-shaped cereal on the back half of the cupcake. Explain that these are the scales of the fish. Add one piece of cereal for the eye, two pieces of cereal on the sides for the lips, and two sugar wafer cookies to the back of the cupcake for the tail.

I Caught a Fish Alive

Movement Activity

1, 2, 3, 4, 5

(Hold up five fingers and count each one.)

I caught a fish alive.

(Pretend to hold a fish.)

6, 7, 8, 9, 10.

(Hold up other five fingers and count each one.)

I let it go again.

(Pretend to throw the fish back into the water.)

Why did I let it go?

(Hold up hands and shrug shoulders.)

Because it bit my finger so!

(Shake right hand.)

Which finger did it bite?

(Hold up right hand.)

The little finger on the right.

(Hold up little finger.)

Traditional

Name: _____ Date: _____

Sizes of Fish

Color the large fish orange.

Color the medium fish blue.

Color the small fish red.

Name: _____ Date: _____

Fish Suncatcher Pattern

Cut two of the fish patterns from contact paper. Peel the backing off the contact paper and lay both pieces with the sticky side up. Stick pieces of colored tissue paper onto one piece of contact paper. Place the other piece of contact paper on top with the sticky sides together. Seal the edges. Punch a hole close to the edge. String a piece of yarn through the hole and hang the suncatcher in a window.

Name: _____ Date: _____

Fill the Aquarium

Count and color 10 of the fish shown at the bottom of the page. Cut out those ten fish and glue them in the aquarium.

  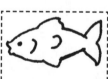  

August

Sunday	Monday	Tuesday	Wednesday	Thursday	Friday	Saturday

Farm Animals

━━━━━━━━━━━━━━━━━ **DAY 1** ━━━━━━━━━━━━━━━━━

Sharing Time: Ask the children if any of them live or have ever lived on a farm. If possible, take a field trip to a farm.

Movement Activity: Have students practice "Old MacDonald Had a Farm" (page 287) all week.

Lesson: Counting Animals

> **Materials:** colored pencils, copies of page 288

> **Directions:** Have the children count the animals in each box. Write the number that shows how many animals there are in each box. Then color all of the animals.

━━━━━━━━━━━━━━━━━ **DAY 2** ━━━━━━━━━━━━━━━━━

Game: Old MacDonald Says

Play this game like Simon Says using Old MacDonald's name instead of Simon's.

━━━━━━━━━━━━━━━━━ **DAY 3** ━━━━━━━━━━━━━━━━━

Lesson: Lost Cow

> **Materials:** colored pencils, copies of page 289

> **Directions:** Have the children draw a line to show how the cow can find its way home to the barn. Then let them color the picture.

━━━━━━━━━━━━━━━━━ **DAY 4** ━━━━━━━━━━━━━━━━━

Sharing Time: Bring the week all together and finish talking about farms and farm animals.

Lesson: Old MacDonald's Farm Mobile

> **Materials:** watercolors, scissors, yarn and hole punch, copies of pages 290 and 291

> **Directions:** Have the children use watercolors to paint the mobile pieces. Then have them cut out the pieces, punch holes, and use yarn to connect them to the barn.

━━━━━━━━━━━━━━━━━ **DAY 5** ━━━━━━━━━━━━━━━━━

Cooking Experience: Pigs in Blankets

> **Materials:** cookie sheet, cooking spray, paper plates, package of hot dogs, can of biscuits and cheese slices (optional)

> **Directions:** Cut each hot dog into two pieces. If desired, cut each slice of cheese into two triangles. Have students stretch the biscuits to make the "blankets." Tell them to hide a piece of hot dog and cheese inside their biscuits. Have them pretend that the hot dog is the pig. Place the pigs in the blankets on a cookie sheet covered with cooking spray. Bake them at 350 degrees Fahrenheit (175 degrees Celsius) for 12 minutes. Allow them to cool before serving.

Old MacDonald's Farm Song

Movement Activity

Old MacDonald had a farm, E - I - E - I - O
And on his farm he had a cow, E - I - E - I - O
With a moo-moo here and a moo-moo there,
Here a moo, there a moo, everywhere a moo-moo
Old MacDonald had a farm, E - I - E - I - O.
Old MacDonald had a farm, E - I - E - I - O
And on his farm he had a sheep, E - I - E -I - O
With a baa-baa here and a baa-baa there
Here a baa, there a baa, everywhere a baa-baa
Old MacDonald had a farm, E - I - E - I - O.
Old MacDonald had a farm, E - I - E - I - O
And on his farm he had a cat, E - I - E - I - O
With a meow-meow here and a meow-meow there
Here a meow, there a meow, everywhere a meow-meow
Old MacDonald had a farm, E - I - E - I - O.
Old MacDonald had a farm, E - I - E - I - O
And on his farm he had a duck, E - I - E - I - O
With a quack-quack here and a quack-quack there
Here a quack, there a quack, everywhere a quack-quack
Old MacDonald had a farm, E - I - E - I - O.
Old MacDonald had a farm, E - I - E - I - O
And on his farm he had a pig, E - I - E - I - O
With an oink-oink here and an oink-oink there
Here an oink, there an oink, everywhere an oink-oink
Old MacDonald had a farm, E - I - E - I - O.
(Pretend to be each of the animals in the song.)

Traditional Song

Name: _____ Date: _____

Counting Animals

Count the animals in each box. Write the number that shows how many animals there are in each box. Then color all of the animals.

Name: _____ Date: _____

Lost Cow

Draw a line to show the cow how to get home to the barn. Then color the picture.

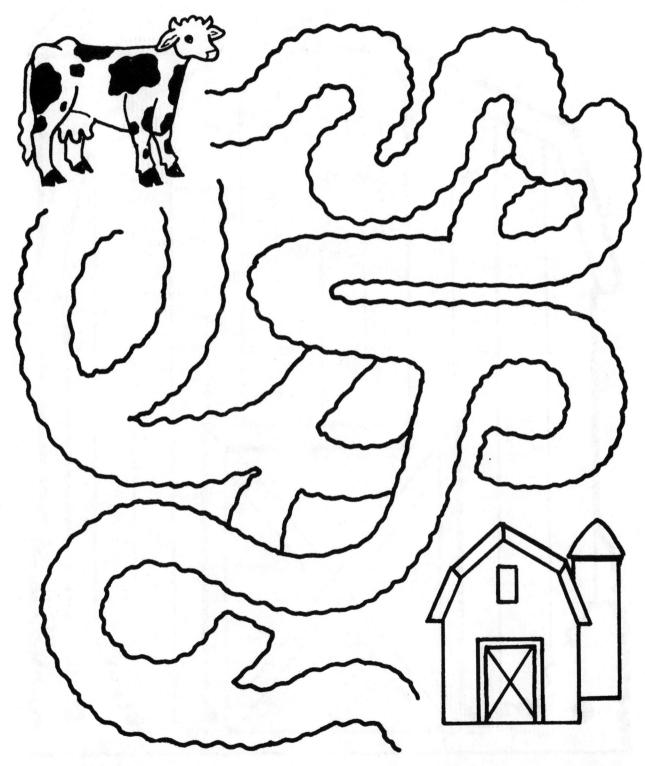

Name: _____ Date: _____

Old MacDonald's Farm Mobile

Old MacDonald's Farm

Name: _____ Date: _____

Old MacDonald's Farm Mobile (cont.)

Paint the animals using watercolors. Cut them out. Punch a hole in each mobile piece where shown. String a piece of yarn through each hole. Tie the yarn onto the barn (page 290).

Fruit Harvest

DAY 1

Sharing Time: Bring in different kinds of fruit. Have the children look at, feel, smell, and taste the fruit. Make a graph that shows the children's favorite type of fruit.

Lesson: Fruit Shadows

  Materials: crayons, copies of page 293

  Directions: Have the children draw a line to match each fruit with its shadow.

DAY 2

Sharing Time: Visit a fruit stand or a fruit orchard. If this is not possible, take the children to a grocery store to look at the different kinds of fruit they have.

Game: Fruit Hunt

Hide different kinds of plastic fruit in a sandbox. Allow the children to hunt for the fruit. The winner is the child who finds the most fruit.

DAY 3

Sharing Time: Continue talking about different kinds of fruit and how they are different in the sizes and textures.

Lesson: The Different Fruit

  Materials: markers or crayons, copies of page 294

  Directions: Have the children look at the fruit in each row. Draw a circle around the fruit that is different. Then color the fruit that is not circled.

DAY 4

Sharing Time: Talk about all the different fruits the children have touched and tasted all week. See if their choice of favorite or least favorite fruit has changed.

Lesson: Fruit Collage

  Materials: magazines with pictures of fruit, colored pencils, markers, scissors, glue, construction paper

  Directions: Have the children either draw or cut out pictures of their favorite fruits and glue them onto a piece of paper to make a fruit collage.

DAY 5

Cooking Experience: Fruit Kabobs

  Materials: long wooden skewers, paper plates, bite-size pieces of fruit, such as bananas, strawberries, grapes, and apples

  Directions: Have some different kinds of fruit-flavored yogurts to use as dips. Cut up the fruit into bite-size pieces. Give each child a paper plate, wooden skewer, and some fruit. Have the children put the fruit on the skewer and lay it on the plate. Help them pour the yogurt over the skewer. Caution them not to stab themselves on the skewers when they eat the fruit.

Name: _____ Date: _____

Fruit Shadows

Draw a line to match each fruit with its shadow. Then color the fruit on the left.

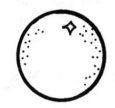

Name: _____ Date: _____

The Different Fruit

Look at the fruit in each row. Draw a circle around the fruit that is different. Then color the fruit that is not circled.

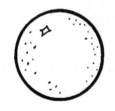 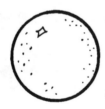 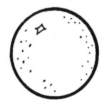  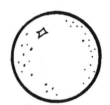

Vegetable Harvest

DAY 1

Sharing Time: With summer almost over, discuss how farmers are harvesting their crops.

Lesson: Counting Vegetables

    Materials: colored pencils, copies of page 296

    Directions: Have the children count the vegetables in each box. Tell them to circle the number that shows how many vegetables are in each box and color the vegetables.

DAY 2

Sharing Time: Explain that sometimes wild and domesticated animals will eat crops.

Lesson: Animals Find Food

    Materials: colored pencils, copies of page 297

    Directions: Have the children trace the lines from the animals to their food.

Game: Pass the Vegetable and Hunt the Vegetable

Use a real or plastic vegetable for Pass the Vegetable. Play the game like hot potato.

DAY 3

Sharing Time: If possible, visit a farm or someone's garden to help harvest the vegetables.

Lesson: Harvesting Vegetables

    Materials: crayons, scissors, glue, copies of page 298

    Directions: Have the children color and cut out the vegetables shown at the bottom of the page. Then have them glue the vegetables in the basket.

DAY 4

Sharing Time: Have the children tell what kinds of vegetables they like and don't like. Have some different kinds of vegetables for them to try.

Lesson: Vegetable Painting

    Materials: white butcher paper; tempera paints, various colors; vegetable chunks; aprons

    Directions: Have the children stamp vegetable chunks dipped in tempera paint on the white butcher paper to make a vegetable mural.

DAY 5

Cooking Experience: Biscuits and Honey Butter

    Materials: cookie sheet, cooking spray, cans of biscuits; clean empty small baby food jars with lids (one jar per two children), heavy whipping cream, honey, measuring cups, measuring spoons

    Directions: Have the children put their biscuits on the cookie sheet and set them aside while making the honey butter. Pour ⅛ cup (30 mL) whipping cream into each jar, add 1 teaspoon (5 mL) of honey. Make sure to tightly close the lids on the jars. Let pairs of children take turns shaking the jars up and down. When they see the lump of butter, in about 15 minutes, have them take off the lid and pour out the extra cream. While the children are shaking the jars of cream and honey, bake the biscuits at 350° Fahrenheit (175° Celsius) for 8 minutes. Have the children put the honey butter on the warm biscuits.

Name: _____ Date: _____

Counting Vegetables

Count the vegetables in each box. Circle the number that shows how many
vegetables are in each box. Then color the vegetables.

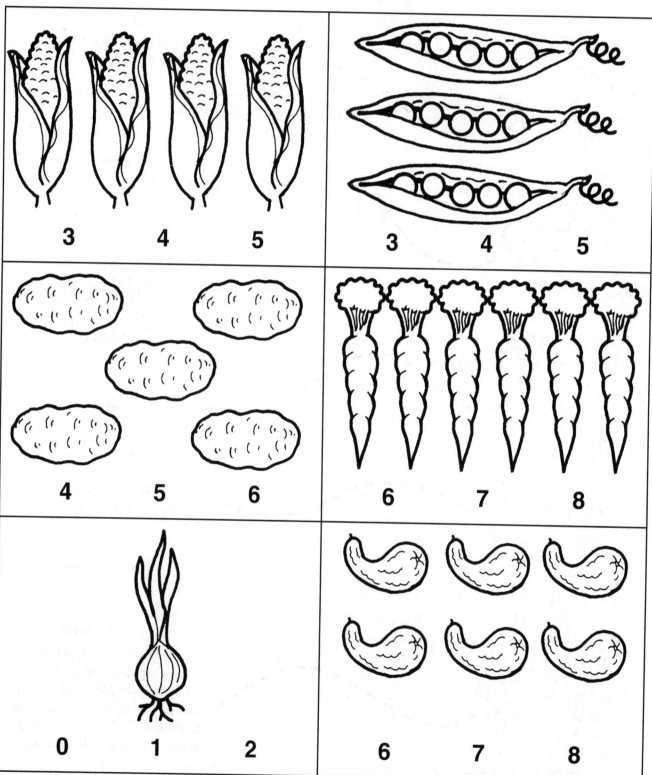

Name: _____ Date: _____

Animals Find Food

Trace the lines from the animals to their food. Then color the pictures.

Name: _____ Date: _____

Harvesting Vegetables

Color and cut out the vegetables shown at the bottom of the page. Then glue the vegetables in the basket.

Back to School

DAY 1

Sharing Time: This week should be filled with outdoor activities and be fun for the children. Have the children tell what they like to do outside. Ask them to tell what their favorite things to do in the summer are. In addition, have the children talk about the different shapes of balloons.

Lesson: Balloon Shapes

>   **Materials:** markers, copies of page 300

>   **Directions:** Have students trace the strings
>   from children to the balloons. Then invite them to color the picture.

DAY 2

Lesson: Sun Shadows

>   **Materials:** construction paper; small objects, such as rocks, sticks, and blocks

>   **Directions:** Give each child a sheet of construction paper. Have the children put different objects on the paper. Then have them leave these in the sun for a few hours. Later take the objects off the paper. Ask the children to describe what happened.

DAY 3

Sharing Time: Talk to the children about animals and their homes and where they live. Talk about the kinds of homes that the children live in.

Lesson: Where Do I Live?

>   **Materials:** crayons, colored pencils or markers, copies of page 301

>   **Directions:** Have the children draw a line to match each animal with its home.

DAY 4

Sharing Time: Collect large furniture or appliance boxes. Invite the children to describe the kinds of homes they live in and what their beds look like. Have them use the boxes to make a house. Cut doors and windows in the boxes. Allow the children to decorate the outside of the boxes in any way they choose.

DAY 5

Cooking Experience: Homemade Ice Cream

>   **Materials:** per two children — 3 lb (1350 g) coffee can with lid; 1 lb. (450 g) coffee can with lid; plastic bowls; plastic spoons; measuring cups; measuring spoons; 1 cup (250 mL) whipping cream; 1 cup (250 mL) milk; ½ cup (125 mL) sugar; 1 teaspoon (5 mL) vanilla or other extract; crushed ice; rock salt; chopped fruit, such as bananas or strawberries (optional)

>   **Directions:** Help the children measure and pour the whipping cream, milk, sugar, and extract into the small can. Add the fruit if desired. Put the small can inside the large can. Fill the space between the cans with crushed ice and add rock salt. Carefully put the lids on the cans. Have two children roll the cans back and forth between them as fast as they can. Check the ice cream every 15 minutes to see if it's thick enough. Add ice and salt, as needed. Soft serve ice cream should be ready in about 30–45 minutes. Then scoop it into the plastic bowls and serve.

Name: _____ Date: _____

Balloon Shapes

Trace the strings from children to the balloons. Then color the picture.

Name: _____ Date: _____

Where Do I Live?

Draw a line to match each animal with its home. Then color the pictures.

Bibliography

Adams, Adrieanne. *The Easter Egg Artists.* Scribner/Scrobmer, 1976.

Asch, Frank. *Bear Shadow.* Prentice-Hall, 1984.

Barton, Byron. *I Want to Be an Astronaut.* HarperCollins, 1997.

Bedford, Annie. *Frosty the Snowman.* Golden Books, 1950.

Berenstain, Stan & Jan. *The Big Honey Hunt.* Random House, 1962.

Brett, Jan. *The Mitten.* G.P. Putnam & Sons, 1989.

Brown, Marc. *Arthur Meets the President.* Little, Brown & Co., 1991.

Brown, Margaret Wise. *Big Red Barn.* HarperCollins, 1965.

Bulla, Clyde. *Robert, What Makes a Shadow?* HarperCollins, 1994.

Carle, Eric. *1, 2, 3, to the Zoo.* Putnam Publishers, 1982.

Carle, Eric. *The Grouchy Ladybug.* Harper Collins, 1996.

Carle, Eric. *Little Cloud.* Philomel Books, 1996.

Carle, Eric. *The Tiny Seed.* Picture Book St., 1987.

Carle, Eric. *The Very Hungry Caterpillar.* Philomel Books, 1987.

Cole, Henry. *Jack's Garden.* Greenwillow Books, 1995.

Gibbons, Gail. *Sun Up, Sun Down.* Harcourt Brace, 1983.

Haywood, Linda. *The First Thanksgiving.* Random House, 1990.

Heller, Ruth. *The Reason for a Flower.* Grosset Dunlap, 1983.

Hutchins, Pat. *Goodnight Owl.* Simon & Schuster, 1972.

Jackson, Kim. *First Day of School.* Troll Cummuns, 1997.

John, Joyce, illus. *The Leprechaun's Treasure.* Nystrom, 1992.

Johnson, Jean. *Postal Workers: A to Z.* Walker, 1987.

Keats, Ezra Jack. *The Snowy Day.* Viking, 1962.

Kellogg, Steven. *Johnny Appleseed.* Morrow Junior, 1988.

Kennedy, Jimmy. *The Teddy Bear's Picnic.* Holt, 1992.

Kindley, Jeff. *Scamper's Year.* Bantam & Dell, 1997.

Kroll, Steven. *It's Groundhog Day.* Holiday House, 1987.

Kroll, Steven. *Will You Be My Valentine?* Holiday House, 1992.

Martin, Bill, Jr. *Brown Bear, Brown Bear, What Do You Hear?* Holt, 1996.

Marzollo, Jean. *I'm a Caterpillar.* Scholastic, 1997.

May, Robert L. *Rudolph the Red Nosed Reindeer.* Applewood Books, 1990.

Mogensen, Jan. *Teddy in the Undersea Kingdom.* G. Stevens Pub., 1985.

Moore, Clement C. *The Night Before Christmas.* Random House, 1975.

Piper, Watty. *The Little Engine That Could.* Platt & Munk, 1961.

Rockwell, Anne. *Fire Engines.* Dutton, 1986.

Seuss, Dr. *Green Eggs and Ham.* Random House, 1960.

Seuss, Dr. *One Fish Two Fish Red Fish Blue Fish.* Random House, 1960.

Tafuri, Nancy. *I Love You, Little One.* Scholastic, 1997.

Williams, Linda. *The Little Old Lady Who Was Not Afraid of Anything.* Crowell Jr. Books, 1986.

Skills Index

Skills Index *(cont.)*

Letter Recognition/Formation
Color the Dinosaur — 34
Color the Turkey — 98
Festival of Lights — 108
German Cornucopia — 249
Igloo Letters — 143
Ladybug Letters — 206
Letter Birds — 220
Matching Kites — 179
Matching Letters — 63
Rudolph — 111
Sun Letters! — 226
Teepee Letters — 82

Listening/Following Directions
Color the Dinosaur — 34
Erupting Volcano — 37
Fall Colors — 48
Teddy Bear Numbers — 49
Apple and Worm Patterns — 56
Painting with Apples — 57
Totem Pole — 83
Plymouth Rock — 87
Indian Corn Magnet Pattern — 89
Horn of Plenty Mobile — 90, 91
I Am Thankful for.... — 96
Color the Turkey — 98
Bells and Stars — 102
Rudolph — 111
Presents — 116
Weather Wheel — 122, 123
Snowflake Mobile — 134
Winter Snow Person — 137
Inuit — 142
Letters to Mail — 153
The Queen of Hearts — 158
Biographies — 161
Lincoln's Story — 162
Up and Down — 181, 182
Ladybug's Favorite Number — 208
Butterfly Life Cycle — 211, 212
Butterfly Mobile — 215
What a Plant Needs to Grow — 228, 229
Mary's Garden — 239
Watercolor Lantern — 258
Summer Fun Visor — 265
My Starfish — 272
Sand Castle and Starfish Mobile — 273
Fish Suncatcher Pattern — 283

Money Recognition/Concepts
Money — 184
Toy Store — 185
Yard Sale — 186

Numbers/Counting
April Numbers — 198
April Showers — 197
Bells and Stars — 102
Birds Everywhere — 217
Coloring Snowflakes — 133
Counting Animals — 288
Counting Jack-O'lanterns — 68
Counting Seashells — 267
Counting Vegetables — 296

Dinosaur Count — 35
Easter Candy — 191
Easter Eggs — 190
The Eight Lost Reindeer — 113
Eight Reindeer — 112
Fill the Aquarium — 284
Find the Stars — 103
Finding Seashells — 269
Fire Trucks — 61
Fishbowl — 268
Five Stars — 104
George Washington's Cherry Tree — 163
Help with the Pies — 88
Honeybees — 201
How Many? — 69
How Many Apples? — 54
How Many Suns? — 225
Ladybug Numbers — 207
The Leprechaun's Gold — 176
Matching Numbers — 50
Matching Starfish — 271
My Phone Number — 172
Nests and Eggs — 219
Nut Hunt — 75
Owl Counting — 77
Presents — 116
Seven Snowflakes — 132
Snow Person Search — 139
Storing Food — 74
Summertime Food — 263
Teddy Bear Numbers — 49
Three Little Apples — 55
Turkeys — 97
Where Are the Ladybugs? — 205

Self-Concept
Happy and Sad Faces — 157
I Am Special Book — 25
Junior Firefighter Badge — 62
Look at Me, I'm Special — 24
Mailbox and Family — 150
My Phone Number — 172
The Way to School — 23
What Hansel and Gretel Saw! — 251

Shape Recognition
Bells and Stars — 102
Circle Trains — 29
Counting Jack-O'-Lanterns — 68
Erupting Volcano — 37
Feed the Hungry Brontosaurus! — 42
Find the Stars — 103
I Think I Can Train — 30

Size Discrimination
Groundhog Sizes — 146
Letters to Mail — 153
Sizes — 232
Sizes of Fish — 282

Spatial Relations
Growing Fruits and Vegetables — 235
Up and Down — 181, 182

Visual Discrimination
Animal Shadows — 147

Counting Vegetables — 296
The Different Fruit — 294
Different Fruits and Vegetables — 236
Easter Eggs — 190
The Eight Lost Reindeer — 113
Finding Mittens — 128
Floating Ghosts — 70
Fruit Shadows — 293
Fruits and Vegetables — 234
Hatching Baby Dinosaurs — 43
Igloo Letters — 143
Kittens' Lost Mittens — 127
Match the Birds — 218
Matching Kites — 179
Matching Letters — 63
Matching Letters and Stamps — 152
Matching Numbers — 50
Matching Skills — 164
Matching Snowflakes — 131
Matching Starfish — 271
Nut Hunt — 75
Object Hunt — 138
Piñatas that Match — 254
The Postal Service — 151
Same and Different Dinosaurs — 41
Snow Person Search — 139
Storing Food — 74
Summertime Food — 263
Sun Letters! — 226
Teepee Letters — 82
Ways to Travel — 246
What's Missing? — 245